Hurricane
at War

Hurricane at War

CHAZ BOWYER

LONDON

IAN ALLAN LTD

To the permanent memory of Flight
Lieutenant Geoffrey 'Sammy' Allard, DFC, DFM
— and all other 'Trenchard Brats' who gave
their lives defending their birthright.

First published 1974

Reprinted 1976

ISBN 0 7110 0564 8

Published by Ian Allan Ltd, Shepperton, Surrey,
and printed in the United Kingdom by
A. Wheaton & Co, Exeter

Contents

Foreword
BY GROUP CAPTAIN T. P. GLEAVE, CBE

Some writers with good reason have drawn an analogy between Sopwith's Camel of World War I and Sydney Camm's Hawker Hurricane of World War II. Each of these fighters was the mainstay of the Royal Air Force in its day, and both achieved great success and gained the affection of those who flew them. And incidentally each had a more glamorous sister to vie with it for the favours of 'suitors' writing subsequent aviation history—the dainty S.E.5a vis-à-vis the snub-nosed pugnacious Camel, and Mitchell's graceful Supermarine Spitfire vis-à-vis the rugged broad-shouldered Hurricane. There that particular analogy ends, because nothing the Camel and S.E.5a achieved in World War I can equal the lethal partnership formed by the Hurricane and Spitfire in the Battle of Britain in World War II when fighting in unison they did so with such devastating effect, and with such a decisive result.

After the Battle of Britain these two famous fighters more or less parted company each going its own way and choosing different paths. As the war progressed the performance of the Spitfire rose as each Mark was succeeded by another, with extensive redesign in the later stages, and in the roles it filled of fighter, fighter-bomber and air reconnaissance it had several very worthy contenders for equal merit in the enemy as well as in the Allied air forces. On the other hand the Hurricane, retaining its basic design to the end, fulfilled an ever-increasing number and variety of roles in virtually every conceivable department of air warfare and in almost every theatre of war, and some writers claim that in this versatility it proved itself unique, that it has no analogy, and no contender for equal merit. I believe this to be true. Perhaps when you have read Chaz Bowyer's fascinating pictorial account of the *Hurricane at War*, interlaced as it is with the experiences of some of those who flew this great fighter on widely differing tasks in many lands, you will think so, too. You will certainly agree that the Hurricane was true to its name—to the enemy's great discomfort it 'raised the dust' wherever and whenever it appeared!

Introduction

The Hawker Hurricane, on its initial introduction to the Royal Air Force, gained instant fame as the first-ever fighter in RAF operational use to exceed 300mph in level flight; and will always be remembered for its major part in the defeat of the Nazi Luftwaffe over England in 1940, during the desperate struggle now known as the Battle of Britain. If these achievements were not sufficient to seal its superb reputation, the post-1940 world-wide service of the Hurricane would be ample to justify the inclusion of its name in any short list of the world's greatest fighter aircraft.

The background to the Hurricane's origin almost epitomises the pre-1939 ultra conservative attitude taken by officialdom to the air defence of Britain. It also exemplifies the foresight and determination of individual British manufacturers to produce the aircraft considered essential to that defence, despite lack of initial official backing or encouragement. In August 1933 Sydney Camm, Hawker's chief designer, had completed a four-gun biplane fighter to the official specification F 7/30, but (like many contemporary manufacturers) was personally convinced that the ultimate in biplane design was almost reached. Accordingly, privately, he commenced design of a fighter in monoplane configuration in October of that same year. On December 5th, 1933, a three-view drawing was completed and discussed in detail with Captain Liptrot, then in charge of the Air Ministry Performance Section. In the following month the design was altered to incorporate a new engine, the Rolls-Royce PV12—later immortalised by the name Merlin—and in March 1934 stressing calculations of the new monoplane were begun. In May drawings were started in the Hawker Drawing Office, whilst in June a one-tenth scale model of the proposed fighter was built especially for testing in the National Physics Laboratory's compressed air tunnel. Finally, on September 4th, 1934, the design was submitted to the Air Ministry. Though still awaiting official reaction, Hawkers went ahead with progressing the aircraft, and first drawings were issued to their experimental shop on October 17th, 1934. A conference, which included Air Ministry representatives, was held on the wooden mock-up at Kingston on January 10th, 1935, and on February 21st, Hawkers received an Air Ministry contract for the construction of one 'high speed monoplane', serial number K5083, to be built to the design submitted in the previous September, and to meet the requirements of Air Ministry Specification F.36/34. On November 6th, 1935, with Hawkers' chief test pilot, George Bulman, at the controls, K5083, the first prototype, made its first brief flight from Brooklands aerodrome. Further flight testing was carried out in February 1936 at RAF Martlesham Heath, and on June 3rd the Air Ministry finally placed a contract with Hawkers for 600 of the new fighters. On June 27th the Ministry also sanctioned officially the name *Hurricane* for the new monoplane. The first production Hurricane, L1547, made its first flight on October 12th, 1937, and within 15 months of that occasion 111 Squadron RAF began receiving its initial equipment of Hurricanes—the first RAF unit to do so. By September 3rd, 1939, the RAF had a total of 18 squadrons equipped with Hurricanes—exactly twice as many as Spitfire units.

It was the Hurricane which bore the brunt of the first eight months of war in France and, indeed, the few Hurricane squadrons there gave the all-conquering Luftwaffe its first bitter taste of RAF opposition. Following the collapse of France came the Battle of Britain—a period now generally recognised as encompassing operations throughout July to October 1940—and during which a total of 1,715 Hurricanes were flown in combat, more than the total of *all* other RAF fighters involved in the conflict. These claimed almost 80 per cent of RAF victories during that fateful summer and autumn. On July 1st the RAF had 29 Hurricane units and 19 Spitfire squadrons; while the main three Fighter Command Groups, 10, 11 and 12, showed an order of battle on July 7th which included 22 Hurricane units and only 13 equipped with Spitfires. Two months later, at the peak of the battle, a total of 30 Hurricane units were complemented by 18 Spitfire and 10 'other fighters' squadrons. Such broad statistics illustrate readily the debt owed to the Hurricanes and their crews during that epic defence. In the following years, 1941–1945, Hurricanes continued to give splendid service in every possible theatre of operations throughout the world, and in virtually every role possible for a single-engined fighter. Abyssinia, Egypt, Libya, Greece, Crete, Malta, Aden, Tunisia, Palestine, Syria, Russia, Italy, Sicily, Iceland, North Atlantic, India, Burma, Java, Sumatra—all were proud battle honours for the ubiquitous Hurricane.

It should be apparent from the foregoing brief summary that no author could properly claim a single book as being in any way adequate to offer a fully complete historical survey of the Hurricane and its many, many facets and achievements. Certainly, that is not claimed for this book. Rather I have attempted, by a collection of verbatim, private accounts and specifically selected illustrations, to at least provide the authentic 'atmosphere' of Hurricane operations in various major and minor contexts. Although such a treatment has meant necessarily compressing some of the Hurricane's most important contributions to the war into merely one man's experience,

collectively they are offered as a genuine tribute to an extraordinary fighter, and no less a recognition of the courage and prowess of the men who served with Hurricanes in war.

In seeking suitable illustrations for these narratives, I was helped enormously by the individual contributors themselves. Long-stored photo albums were unearthed and dusted off to provide me with many of the privately-taken photographs used in this book. A simple thank you to such generosity seems inadequate, but is offered sincerely to each. Of the other illustrations, I am indebted yet again to the unselfish and willing help of many close friends and acquaintances. Ann Tilbury of *Flight International* provided her normal, unstinting assistance, not to mention charm and occasional cups of tea. Ted Hine of the Imperial War Museum could hardly have been more helpful. Peter Robertson and the Photographic Archives staff of the Canadian Public Archives, Ottawa, provided not only excellent photos but superb co-operation to a stranger. Equally generous in so many ways with aid and expert advice were Chris Ashworth, Norman L. R. Franks, R. Elias, 'Jeff' Jefford, Alfred Price, Chris Shores, Les Southern, Geoff Thomas, Richard Leask Ward. To all of them I owe a sincere debt of thanks. I am also very much indebted to Mr. M. Ross for his permission to quote the log-book of his brother, the late Flight Lieutenant J. K. Ross, DFC; to Miss Kerry Hood of Victor Gollancz for permission to use an extract from the late Wing Commander Ian Gleed's book, *Arise To Conquer*; and by no means least am I indebted to Group Captain Tom Gleave for so generously volunteering to write the Foreword to this book.

Chaz Bowyer
Norwich, 1974

The prototype Hurricane, K5083, known originally as the 'F.36/34 Single-Seater Fighter - High Speed Monoplane', in pristine silver sheen, after testing trials at RAF Martlesham Heath, February 1936, with armament and radio installed, and large production-style radiator bath.

First of the Many

Far left: Two's company. K5083, the first-ever Hurricane, with Flight Lieutenant P. W. S. 'George' Bulman, MC, AFC at the controls (in casual trilby hat. . .), keeps company with another prototype and stable-mate, K5115, the first Hawker Henley. The latter made its initial flight on March 24th, 1937.

Left: Sir Sydney Camm, CBE, FRAeS, Director of Design, Hawker Siddeley Aviation Limited (as he became)—the man responsible for design of the Hurricane. Born in Windsor on August 5th, 1893, Camm first joined the H. G. Hawker Engineering Company in 1923, was appointed chief designer two years later, knighted in 1953 for his outstanding services to British aviation, and died on March 12th, 1966.

Far left: The Office. Part-view of the cockpit of an early Hurricane I. Of particular interest here are the crash pad fixed to the ring gunsight, gun button in the control column spade grip, compass (below the centre instrument panel), seat raise/lower handle, and emergency hand pump for flaps and undercarriage (right).

Left: Dashboard. Pilot's panorama in a Hurricane I. Starting from bottom left, anti-clockwise: engine starter; ignition switches; three switches for navigation lights and gun bearings heating; altimeter; gyro compass; turn & bank indicator; oil temperature; radiator temperature; fuel indicator; oil and petrol pressure (to left, in white cover); above latter, super-charger pressure gauge; to right, petrol tanks change-over switches; top right, right, gunsight illumination; engine revs counter; top right of central panel, rate of climb indicator; centre top, artificial horizon (for 'blind flying'); centre left, airspeed indicator; above, (marked P & S) undercarriage dial; top left, undercarriage warning buzzer; below, two gauges for oxygen supply and relevant pressure; below latter, clock; to left of clock, emergency boost. Gunsight bracket (top centre) is empty here but the sorbo crash pad for protection of the pilot's face is evident. The large bracket at left of photo was for installation of the camera film indicator.

Below: Exploiting the design's superb manoeuvrability here is L1648, one of the first 600-aircraft batch to be contracted. In 1940 this particular machine served with 85 Squadron.

Right: Later production version, displaying to advantage the wide track undercarriage of the design. Other improvements evident here include ejector-type exhaust stubs, anti-spin fillet added under tail section, and bullet-proof front windscreen. The first Hurricane to be fitted with three-bladed propeller was L1562.

Below right: L1547, the first production Hurricane, which made its first flight on October 12th, 1937, seen here on Brooklands airfield. This machine was eventually lost on October 10th, 1940, when serving with 312 (Czech) Squadron at Speke. Its pilot, Sergeant O. Hanzlicek, baled out but was killed, and the Hurricane crashed into the River Mersey.

Dawn Tableau. An 87
Squadron Hurricane, PD-P,
and its steel-helmeted crew
provide a watchful scene at
Debden during the August
1939 'practice war'—within
a month the real thing had
started.

Into Service
ROY DUTTON

To the pre-war RAF pilots who were first to change their biplane fighters for the immensely more powerful monoplane Hurricanes, the new 'bus' was a mixture of excitement and new-fangled innovations. Roy Dutton was one of the privileged few to gain experience in Hurricanes at that time, being a member of 111 Squadron, the first RAF unit to be equipped. It stood him in good stead during the years 1939 and 1940, when he amassed a total of 911 sorties, fighting through the campaign in France and the Battle of Britain and being credited with at least 19 air victories. He eventually retired as Air Commodore CBE, DSO, DFC.

The first Hurricane received by 111 Squadron arrived in January 1938 and, with a total of some 300 hours flying experience, my first flight in the Hurricane (L1553) was on January 18th and lasted 20 minutes, involving three circuits and landings. I recall that this was a markedly strange experience, the Hurricane being by comparison to the ladylike Gauntlet, a large, powerful, high performance, low-wing monoplane with retractable undercarriage and landing flaps. It may horrify the modern pilot, but for the first flight each pilot was under orders to accomplish three take-offs and landings without retracting the undercarriage, and to keep the cockpit canopy open fully. This was exciting rather than frightening, but in consequence the whole aeroplane shook like the proverbial leaf. The feel was heavy; the draught seemed in keeping with the type-name of the machine, and the noise, speed and sense of power exhilarating, as was the wide open view.

After Squadron Leader John Gillan, the commanding officer, Flying Officer Peter Powell, my Flight commander in A Flight, and Flight Lieutenant Hugh Kennedy, B Flight commander, I think I was about the next one to fly a Hurricane. My memory may play me false, I make no claim, and it is of no matter. But at this time I think we only had three Hurricanes delivered—L1550, L1552 and L1553. L1555, in which John Gillan later made the record, 'down-wind' flight from Edinburgh to Northolt, was yet to come (and to be named 'State Express 555' thereafter), and there

Hurricane 'pioneers'. 111 Squadron's Hurricanes lined up at Northolt just prior to the unit's visit to the Paris Fête de l'Air, which took place on July 9th, 1938. Aircraft identifiable (from front) are L1559, L1560, L1548 and L1552 (total 12 aircraft). In foreground 111's commander, Squadron Leader John Gillan, briefs his pilots. Identification of pilots includes: 1. Plt Off R. G. Dutton, A Flt; 2. Either Sgt W. L. Dymond, A Flt (later awarded DFM and killed in action, September 2nd, 1940), OR Sgt J. T. Craig (later awarded DFM, killed in action after Battle of Britain. 3. Plt Off B. A. Mortimer, B Flt; 4. Plt Off S. D. P. Connors (awarded DFC and killed in action August 18th, 1940); 5. Sqn Ldr J. W. Gillan (OC); 6. Plt Off D. C. Bruce, A Flt; 7. Sgt Gunn, A Flt; 8. Plt Off

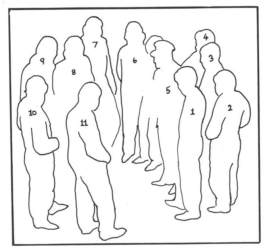

W. B. Skinner, B Flt & squadron adjutant; 9. Plt Off Heath, A Flt; 10. Fg Off R. P. R. Powell, A Flt Cdr; 11. Fg Off C. S. Darwood (killed in action, May 1940 at Seclin, France.)

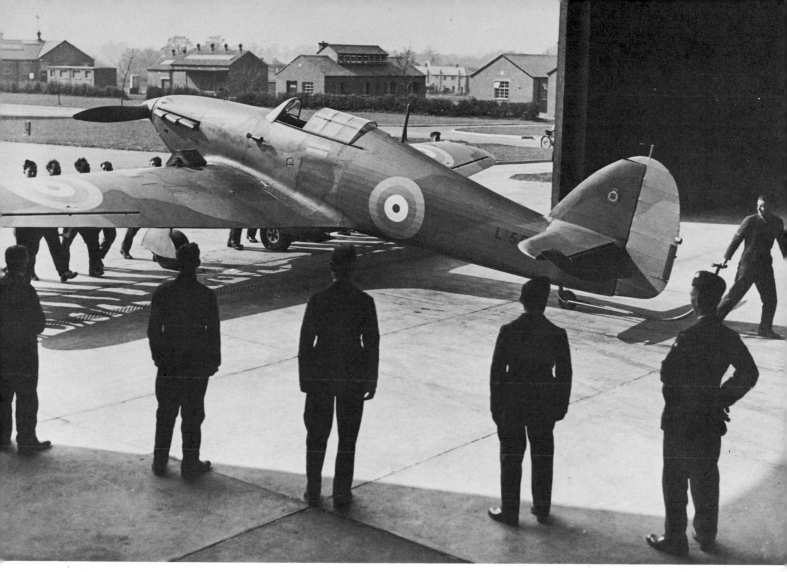

was a queue for every pilot to launch himself—all circuits and bumps being critically observed. I recall that I had no difficulty in somehow making satisfactory arrivals and I was therefore let loose on the following two days which, from my log book, I see was the sum total of my Hurricane flying that month. On the latter two trips of 45 and 30 minutes respectively, we were allowed to retract the undercarriage and close the hood which improved the ride considerably, though I recall that, still not being acclimatised to the new beast, there was an impression of engine vibration and noise. The marked increase in speed in comparison with the Gauntlet also remains in my memory. On those initial trips we were, as I recall, forbidden to try any aerobatics. However, no doubt in keeping with our commanding officer's opinion of his brood being an undisciplined lot, not many of us abided by the injunction and I remember that my first loop

seemed to take up a lot of sky. (I see in my log book that I received the CO's written authority to carry out aerobatics on April 21st, 1938!)

111 Squadron, being the nucleus of the Air Fighting Development Establishment and the first to be equipped with the Hurricane, *ipso facto* proceeded to undertake the Service trials. In consequence, we, as a squadron, had the advantage of accruing some not inconsiderable experience on the type by the time war broke out. For myself, I had in September 1939 almost 400 Hurricane hours, 41 hours being at night. The Rolls-Royce Merlin in those early Hurricanes although reliable did have teething troubles, as did the aeroplanes, and a pretty close liaison with Ronnie Harker of Rolls-Royce, Hucknall and George Bulman and Phillip Lucas of Hawkers, Weybridge was maintained.

The first Mark had the two-bladed wooden propeller, fabric wings and re-

High-speed Hurri. L1555 of 111 Squadron being returned to its hangar at Northolt, 1938. It was in this machine that the squadron commander, John Gillan, flew his famous London–Edinburgh–London two-way flight on February 10th, 1938, achieving an average ground speed of 408.75mph—and, incidentally, acquiring for himself the nickname 'Down-wind' thereafter.

19

tractable tailwheel. At high speeds the wing gun bay panels sometimes partially blew out and the wing fabric distended like sausages between the ribs. On one occasion when in a near-vertical formation dive, I remember being violently rotated and had some difficulty in recovering—my port undercarriage leg had extended. I remember this well because the high air speed made it jam halfway down for good and that was that. Result—the first belly landing in a Hurricane, a bit of a bone-shaker because of the frozen ground at Northolt at the time and the alarming slide with the nose tipped right down due to the position of the ventral-mounted radiator. I remember as I slipped over Western Avenue on the airfield boundary, switching off the ignition in the hope that the propeller would stop horizontal. It didn't it stopped vertical and snapped like a carrot. Such pain as I suffered could, I reflected, have been entirely prevented had I been wearing a cricket 'box', for it

seemed that the entire force of deceleration impinged on the especially tender area of the male anatomy . . . !

With a total of all-but 750 hours on the Hurricane, I only suffered engine failure on three occasions and partial failure once. In April 1938, after taking off from Northolt, and having just tucked my wheels up and heading north toward Ruislip, there was a shattering silence. I doubt that I could have been but a couple of hundred feet up or so and frantically started to hand-pump some flap down before pitching hopefully into the limited bit of mead-owland below and to port. In the somewhat frenzied seconds available I entirely forgot to switch off the ignition, also to turn off the fuel. As things turned out this was fortunate for at about 50 feet up, and in the act of aiming to clear trees and cattle, the engine spluttered into uncertain life and I managed to nurse myself round to through about 200 degrees and flop over the north-west boundary of the airfield, wheels locked

Second RAF squadron to receive Hurricanes was No 3, seen here at Kenley aerodrome preparing for their part in the 1938 Empire Air Day display. Nearest three aircraft in front row are L1576, L1572 and L1569. All aircraft are fitted with the Watts two-blade fixed pitch propellers and kidney-type exhausts.

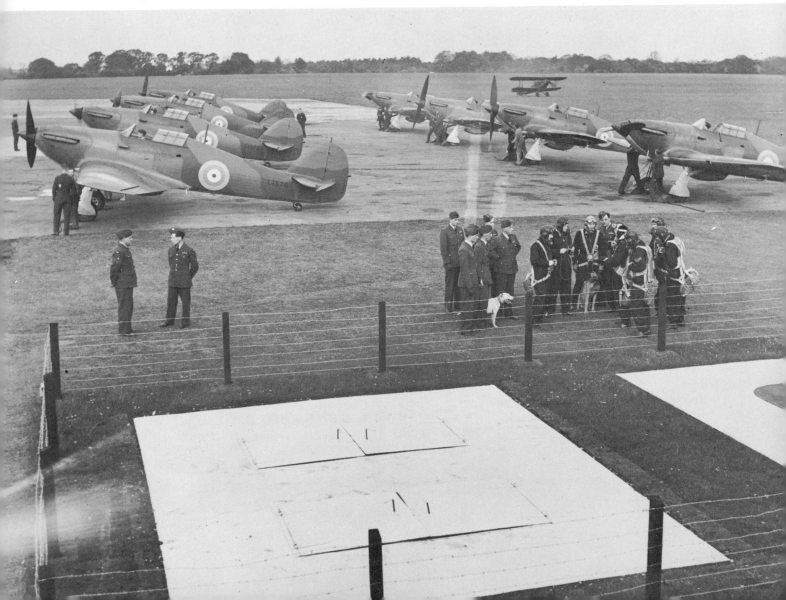

down. How I ever got the wheels locked down I never knew. I never had to pump so hard in my life. The engine then died for good and I could hardly believe that the undercarriage didn't fold up. I don't think we ever found out what caused the failure, but the odd engine cut, although not too common an occurrence, did happen and on taking up this particular machine (L1550) later in the day, it cut again but fortunately before I had lifted off and I managed to swing to port sufficient to obtain enough living space and pull up undamaged.

It was not until about early spring 1940 that improvements such as the three-bladed metal two-pitch propellers began to appear—at any rate, in 111 Squadron—and the limitations in performance of the early Marks showed up in odd ways. (The constant speed Rotol propellers did not appear until 1940.) Not surprisingly take-off time was poor by comparison and the effect of a muddy airfield—in this case, Wick, Caithness on March 21st 1940—caused me another engine failure incident. The big wooden propeller had scooped up the mud and effectively sealed the radiator honeycomb, thus causing overheating and partial seizure very shortly after crossing the coast. Thanks to a gale-force wind on

Above: In April 1938, 56 Squadron became the third unit to begin re-equipment with Hurricanes, based then at North Weald. One of its initial issue aircraft, L1609, is seen here on August 17th, 1939 being refuelled from a triple-hose bowser during that year's air exercises.

Left: Ready to go. Sergeant Brown, B Flight, 111 Squadron, about to climb into his Hurricane. An interesting view of the 1938–39 RAF fighter pilot's clothing.

21

the tail and a modicum of luck, a safe, dead-stick, wheels-down landing was accomplished.

Gauntlet flying ceased in mid-March 1938 and Hurricane trips, until then interspersed, were of short duration—most being of 30 minutes and very few more than an hour. Thus my first night flight in the Hurricane took place on March 15th after 26 hours on the type. I cannot recall whether it was moonlight or not, but the most noticeable thing was the considerable glare from the stub exhausts which seriously affected night vision, and 'blinkers' (anti-glare shields) fitted to the engine cowl were devised and became an early modification. Even with these, flying on dark nights in true blackout conditions and until cruise power could be used, reference to the newfangled Sperry blind flying panel was often necessary after leaving the flare path. It paid to make full use of the Link Trainer when it was introduced and become master of the situation. Fortuitously, I became the squadron blind flying instructor and did the full Link Trainer course at North Weald. Talking of night flying, in early December 1938, my Flight commander, the late Peter Powell, and I were ordered to Sutton Bridge during a moonless period to assess the effects of firing the eight .303 Brownings over the ranges there, and the sparsely populated countryside provided a true replica of the wartime blackout flying to come. I led off, with Peter a second or so behind, and the exhaust glare (as I expected) was such that I had to clamp on to instruments at once. Peter said that it was only my tail and purple formation-keeping lights that kept him safely orientated. The tracers from the guns and the

Luncheon Alfresco. Ground crew of a 79 Squadron Hurricane utilise the tailplane for a hurried snack between alerts in the air defence exercises of August 1939, at Biggin Hill. 79 had received its first Hurricanes in the previous November.

muzzle flash were no problem, only a fascinating experience. Maybe the 20mm cannon yet to come had the bigger punch, but the optimumly-ranged concentration of fire power was reassuring. Indeed, with the De Wilde mixture in the belts, the eight guns closely grouped in two batteries of four guns later proved their efficiency, especially in a dogfight, if not perhaps so lethal against, say a Junkers 88, which seemed to have a considerable capacity to absorb .303 rounds aimed from the rear.

Other than the basic exercises demanded by the flying training syllabus and that involved in developing tactics for attack against bomber targets (undertaken with such new types as the Wellington, Harrow, Hampden, Whitley and Battles), much demonstration air drill and formation aerobatics were undertaken and the few Hurricanes available were in demand at the Empire Air Day displays of 1938 and 1939. Special demonstrations were laid on at Northolt too, for example, VIP foreigners—including the Germans on one occasion! A highlight was the French Fête de l'Air at Villacoublay in July 1938 when, as official guests of the French Government and Air Force, a formation of nine Hurricanes provided a display at the cost of a splendid five days in Paris.

When the war came on September 3rd, 1939, we had already been on a sort of semi-alert since the Munich crisis in 1938, and the Hurricane was by that time fully operational. In 1938 however, if the situation in 111 Squadron was indicative of the situation in other squadrons in Fighter Command, we had a rather limited rearming capability. The fewer Hurricanes in service in 1938 were, moreover, likely to have been a less potent operational force.

Bottom: By the outbreak of war in September 1939, the RAF was not the only air force to have Hurricanes. On September 3rd the Royal Canadian Air Force had a total of 270 aircraft on charge—19 of these were Hurricanes. The first six were in use by February 1939, and one of the earliest, serialled 313, is pictured here flying over Vancouver on April 3rd, 1939. It belonged to 1 Squadron, RCAF.

Wheels up. 32 Squadron takes off from Biggin Hill, early 1939. The unit's pre-1939 letter, KT, are much in evidence.

Blitzkrieg
ROLAND BEAMONT

Scramble. 87 Squadron's pilots demonstrate a 'panic' take-off, France, March 1940. Nearest Hurricane, 'D', is L1774. 87 had by this time been in France for six months, one of its members, Flight Lieutenant R. 'Bobby' Voase-Jeff, having destroyed the first Heinkel III to be brought down in France, on November, 2nd, 1939.

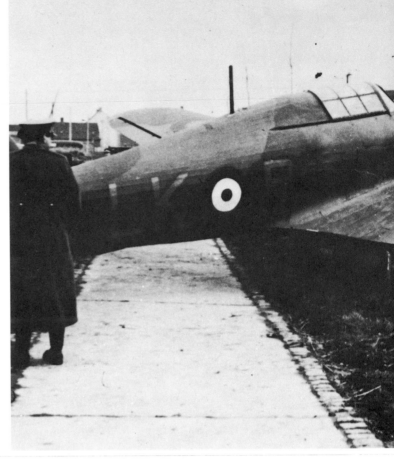

Royal inspection.
HM King George VI
visiting Lille-Seclin
aerodrome on December 6th,
1939. In foreground are
Hurricanes of 85 Squadron
(with white hexagon unit
markings on fins) and three
from 87 Squadron. Facing
these are two Gloster
Gladiators and a Bristol
Blenheim IV.

Being posted to France in October 1939, I could not claim to have an expert opinion on Hurricane operations at that time as I had come straight out from the 11 Group Fighter Pool at St Athan with the impressive total of 130 flying hours, of which 15 were on Hurricanes. But after six months and the 10 days from May 10th, 1940, I could claim to be almost a veteran. 87 Squadron was based on Lille Vendeville aerodrome which consisted of an almost circular field of mud, one large old hangar, a group of wooden huts and an extraordinary monument to Gallic ingenuity in the shape of a towering wrought-iron platform mounted about 20 feet above an enormous iron tank which together did duty as the station latrine. In hot weather this produced an aroma needing experience to be believed, and in the winds, rain, ice and snow—of which we had plenty—its successful use was an exercise in extreme fortitude and dexterity; as so frequently was Hurricane flying in France at that time. The wooden-hutted billets were far from draught-proof and kept little of the fearsome winter of 1939 outside, so that it was

often a relief to climb into the cockpits of our Hurricanes and shut the canopies to keep the wind off.

Flying during the early part of 1940 was restricted due to the tendency for all the airfields in northern France to become water-logged acres of black mud, and on one occasion we had to fly the whole squadron from Lille down to Le Touquet by taking off from the perimeter road as the airfield was in a totally impossible state. To a newcomer the Hurricane was an immensely powerful but not very demanding aeroplane. Its wide track undercarriage, stable and responsive flying characteristics and reliable engine and hydraulic system resulted in a general atmosphere of confidence in the squadron, so that the newcomer had no reason to become apprehensive. Getting lost over the flat, agricultural plain of northern France in the generally unpleasant prevailing weather was perhaps the only recurrent difficulty. But most of the flying consisted of formation practice and occasional patrols against reported enemy reconnaissance activity, and so one flew in sublime con-

Top left: Wing Commander Roland Prosper Beamont, DSO, OBE, DFC, who flew with 87 Squadron throughout the battles of France and Britain, 1940.

Centre: Internee. L1628 of 87 Squadron in which Squadron Leader W. E. Coope force-landed in neutral (then) Belgium on November 4th, 1939. He landed along a main road but was forced to swerve hard to starboard to avoid hitting a petrified civilian cyclist, thus ripping off his right wheel. This was the first of several Hurricanes to be 'interned' in Belgium prior to the German *Blitzkrieg* onslaught of May 1940.

Above: Seen here in France, early 1940, P2617 was first issued to the RAF in January 1940, saw service with No 1 (Canadian) Squadron later that year, and in August 1941 was reported on strength of 9 FTS.

fidence that one's formation leader knew precisely where he was. In the event I suspect that this was seldom the case, and we were very well lost on one occasion when operating from Senan, near Metz, over the Maginot Line in March 1940, and after two hours flying around apparently rather aimlessly we eventually landed at an airfield which turned out to be Metz itself. This airfield was situated at the base of a hill on which Metz stood with a towering steeple near the summit, and when, after my aircraft had been refuelled, I took off to return the short distance to base solo, my engine faltered and cut for a moment during the critical climb-out up the side of the hill over the roofs of Metz. For a brief moment it seemed inevitable that I would have to put down straight ahead amongst the houses, but while bracing for this unpleasant possibility the engine picked up again and the Hurricane climbed laboriously at virtually street level up the high street of Metz into the clear.

At about this time I had my first encounter with the enemy. This occurred one day in February 1940, when based at Le Touquet with 87 after our main airfield at Lille had become inoperable due to continuous rain and slush. We had found Le Touquet a hospitable spot and a champagne party was developing on the morning in question, more or less as a continuation of the previous night's activity, when the Readiness Section was scrambled. This consisted of the Australian Johnny Cock and myself (with about 170 hours total flying time) with fixed pitch Hurricane Is. As we strapped in hurriedly I noted with disapproval that the weather was far from convenient with solid low cloud and drizzle, and I hoped that our unreliable TR9 radios would be of use when wanted. In the event mine was not, but once committed over the cloud sheet in the Somme estuary area we were told to turn north-east and climb fast. Shortly afterwards we were surprised to see the unmistakable shape of a Heinkel III about 2,000 feet above and climbing hard.

He began to fire tracer at us at long range and we were just beginning to close in when the sky turned purple, vision became confused and I had time only to suspect oxygen starvation and push the nose down with controls centralised before virtually losing consciousness. Coming to just above the cloud sheet and feeling

H39, the only Rotol Hurricane to serve with the Belgian Air Force. The pilot here, Van den Hove D'Erstenrÿk (later killed in the Battle of Britain), wrecked the aircraft in March 1940 when force-landing with propeller trouble at Liege-Bierset.

Above right: Posing for the press. Pilots of 73 Squadron go through the motions of a briefing for the benefit of visiting journalists, late 1939. Third pilot from right is Flying Officer Edgar James 'Cobber' Kain, a New Zealander who became the RAF's first five-victory 'ace' of World War II, and was credited with at least 17 victories before his death in an accident on June 7th, 1940.

Right: Back from patrol. Hurricane landing at Vassincourt, France, 1939. Long identified as a machine of 1 Squadron (Fg Off P. P. Hanks), there is now evidence that in fact this was S-Sugar of 73 Squadron, piloted by Sergeant (later Wing Commander) P. V. Ayerst. The full-depth rudder stripes in red/white/ blue were applied to avoid misidentification in the air by other 'friendly' aircraft— particularly French fighters.

decidedly out of contact with what was going on, I opened the canopy for fresh air, felt a jerk and eventually discovered that my oxygen hose was missing, having apparently been disconnected at the bayonet joint where I had failed to check it in the hurry to take off. Then, when calling for a homing over the unbroken cloud sheet, the aforesaid TR9 produced no recognisable assistance and left me to sort out the situation. I decided that a let-down over the sea was the only safe course and carried this out on a south-westerly heading, finally breaking cloud at very low level over a smooth grey sea, and made my way back north along the sand dunes of the French coast to Le Tourquet, where Johnny Cock was already back having thought that he had shot the Heinkel down, or at least seen it disappear diving steeply into the cloud cover.

When all-out war started on May 10th, 1940, the Hurricanes of the Air Component were soon heavily engaged and began to be reinforced from the UK, but they continued to sail into battle in the

immaculate squadron formations of those days and sometimes got clobbered badly in the process. In my second combat, 87 Squadron in three Vics of three, intercepted a formation of Dorniers with Messerschmitt 110 escorts, near Maastricht, and the battle immediately broke up into a mêlée of individual combats. We had been sitting in the ditch by our Hurricanes which served as our Flight dispersal at Lille Marque, and sounds of gun fire and bombs had indicated activity in the direction of Lille, and very high and barely in sight in the afternoon glare was a small white parachute. This turned out to be a pilot of 85 Squadron from Seclin, but we did not see the end of his descent as the operations telephone suddenly shrilled and we were off to patrol Maastricht at 18,000 feet.

The field was too small for the whole squadron to be parked on one side and theoretically one Flight took off after the other, but in this event 12 Hurricanes thundered at each other from opposite ends of the field as they gathered speed

Above right: Neutrals. Belgian-built Hurricanes of the 2nd Escadrille in parade line on the ill-fated Schaffen-Diest airfield, just prior to Germany's lightning invasion of the Low Countries in the spring of 1940. On May 10th this was the sight which greeted Luftwaffe bombers and fighters when they approached from the direction of the woods in the far background. In a matter of minutes the Hurricanes were burning wrecks.

Above far right: Welcome back. Sergeant 'Sammy' Allard is greeted by fellow members of 85 Squadron at Seclin, May 1940, on return from a patrol in which he had destroyed at least two enemy aircraft. In less than two weeks of continuous fighting, Geoffrey Allard accounted for at least 10 German aircraft. He then fought through the Battle of Britain, was commissioned, awarded two DFMS and a DFC, and was credited with 21 victories before his death on March 13th, 1941.

Below right: Stern attack. A Vic of 73 Squadron's Hurricanes demonstrating a line astern attack on a Fairey Battle. At this stage of the air war most RAF fighter units were still adhering to the inflexible pre-1939 combat tactics, but the stern test of actual air fighting soon proved such rigid manoeuvres to be useless—and, too often, fatal.

ponderously behind their huge fixed pitch propellers—a hump in the middle of the field ensuring that no one could judge if someone from the other Flight was on a collision course until both were converging on the hump at a combined speed of about 150mph. But there were no collisions and after a fleeting impression of other aircraft flashing by on either side we were clear and closing into formation in a long climbing turn towards the east. As we joined formation an indistinct radio message indicated activity in the Brussels area, and then directly ahead and a little above was a formation of big aircraft crossing from left to right. 87 continued at full power until I began to recognise the aircraft ahead as a squadron of Dornier 17 bombers.

There was no moment of hesitation. With the gunsight ON and gun button to FIRE, then ruddering the gunsight on to the nearest bomber in a 30 degrees deflection astern attack and opening fire with a long burst. I was still alongside Voase-Jeff's Hurricane and he told me later that I had opened fire 'miles out of range' as he wasn't in range himself and I was behind him! But all that mattered at that point was to get in at the enemy, and then the immediate sky became full of small twin-engined aeroplanes which I recognised as Me 110s. There was no time for tactics or formation drill and I broke into a hard port turn instinctively and saw a 110 go by close behind. A further maximum power turn to port brought me out of the immediate mêlée and then I saw a Hurricane diving away with a 110 close behind him streaming gunfire smoke. He was well out of range of my guns so I started to give chase, when ahead and crossing from right to left appeared a Dornier, its own nose down for home with twin trails of smoke from its full-throttle engines.

I was not able to close the range quickly and we were flying due east and down to 10,000 feet when I realised then I was not gaining much ground. At long range, with one ring vertical deflection, I fired a long burst from the eight Brownings and immediately saw the Dornier's port engine stop with smoke and a sharp yaw. Now I had him and a short burst from close range dead astern put him into a vertical dive into the low cloud at 2,000 feet. Being

almost certainly well into enemy territory by now and alone, and above a revealing white cloud sheet, I began to feel somewhat insecure and so dived through the cloud and turned on to a north-westerly heading over the rolling forests of the Ardennes. Presently the trees gave way to ploughed land and while looking for landmarks I was suddenly bracketed by shell bursts, whether friendly or otherwise I could not determine. This also seemed unhealthy so I dived to low level over the fields to provide a less sitting target and was then slightly shaken to experience tracer fire from behind. A hasty sideslip and quick look over the left shoulder and there, not 200 yards away, was another Dornier with this front gunner having a quite effective go at me.

A full throttle tight left turn at treetop height soon reversed the position and although this German flew his bomber with skill and tenacity in trying to out-manoeuvre my Hurricane, in less than two turns we were coming round on to his tail, then with engine boost over-ride pulled, banking into position for a broad deflection shot. With the Dornier in a perfect position for this at under 200 yards range, and with his top rear gunner now also opening fire, I pressed the gun button.

The price of neutrality. Schaffen-Diest airfield scene after the Luftwaffe's attack on May 10th, 1940. The shattered remains of this Hurricane illustrate a modification built in to most Belgian-built machines—the reinforced crash pylon of the cockpit framework. Due to the soggy grass airfields in use in Belgium at that period, landing and taxying accidents were not infrequent.

Three rounds went off—then silence. Now here was a predicament. I had out-manoeuvred this worthy bomber pilot whose aeroplane was almost as fast as mine at this ground level combat. He had three gun positions with an unknown amount of ammunition remaining, while I had eight guns and no ammunition, and the moment I broke the circle from behind his tail he could jump me again unless I could think up something. Closing in under his tail, and trying to keep between the fields of fire of his upper and lower guns, I used all the Hurricane's manoeuvrability and full over-boost power to roll away to the right from the lefthand circle, and then pushed the nose down to 50 feet above the fields on a northerly heading. Looking round I saw this determined German come round after me to level out some way behind and fire a few more bursts from steadily increasing range. Then as the Hurricane drew away, he pulled up, rocking his wings, before turn-

ing away to the east. I felt he'd scored a moral victory, but I was at least still around to have another go at his friends.

My third combat was a classic example of the weakness of inflexibility. We were now operating full-time from the grass field at Lille Marque and had been ordered off at three-squadron strength to patrol the ground battle area at Valenciennes at 10,000 feet. We made a fine sight as 36 Hurricanes formed up in the late afternoon sun in three squadron boxes, line-astern, four sections of Vic-threes to a squadron. I was flying No. 2 in the right-hand section of 87 Squadron, leading the Wing, and it made one feel quite brave looking back at so many friendly fighters. And then without fuss or drama about 10 Messerschmitt 109s appeared above the left rear flank of our formation out of some high cloud. The Wing leader turned in towards them as fast as a big formation could be wheeled, but the 109s abandoned close drill and, pulling

Aftermath. A poignant view of a wrecked Hurricane on the beach at Dunkirk, scene of the Allied armies' final escape from the overpowering German offensive, May to June, 1940. The battle for France was now over—the Battle of Britain was soon to begin . . .

their turn tight, dived one after the other on to the tail sections of the Wing. Their guns streamed smoke and one by one four Hurricanes fell away. None of us fired a shot—some never even saw it happen—and the enemy disengaged, while we continued to give a massive impression of combat strength over the battle area with four less Hurricanes than when we started. We had had more than three times the strength of the enemy on this occasion and had been soundly beaten tactically by a much smaller unit, led with flexibility and resolution.

The Battle of France was soon over but the authorities were slow to react to facts and change the rules, and change came about the hard way by squadrons learning from experience and adapting themselves. Nevertheless, there were still some squadrons going into action in the beginning of the Battle of Britain in 'standard Fighter Command attacks', and many in the inflexible three-sections Vic formation. In 87 Squadron we had modified our tactics to an initial turn in towards the enemy when sighted, followed by flexible exploitation of the subsequent situation—in other words, every man for himself. We still flew in three Vics of three, but in extended battle formation with wing men weaving for cross reference, and at no time did we practise close No 2 cover, or the basic 'Finger-Four' formation flown by the Germans and adopted by the RAF tardily at the end of the battle. One of the most effective tactics used by our side was the head-on 'into the brown' manoeuvre. One had experience of this on August 15th, 1940 over Portland when, still with 87 Squadron and now flying out of Exeter, Squadron Leader Lovell Grieg led us straight into the starboard front of a dense mass of Junkers 87s, with Me 110s escorting, which the RDF had reported as '120-plus'. We were quite prepared to believe them and our somewhat uncoordinated plunge right through the middle of this armada seemed to put them off their bomb aiming more than somewhat, in addition to destroying a number of them.

In the spring and summer of 1940, although without the elegance and high altitude performance of the Spitfire, the Hurricane was a machine of its time, and many of us would not have changed it for any other mount. We knew it as a rugged, stable, forgiving aeroplane which was tolerant of our clumsiness and the worst that the weather could do. It absorbed legendary amounts of enemy fire and kept flying. We could hit the target well with its eight guns and when in trouble we felt that we could outfly the enemy's best. The Hurricane and the Spitfire made a great team, but I never regretted my posting to a Hurricane squadron in that fateful time.

Battle of Britain

Getting ready. 111 Squadron refuelling at Wick, early 1940. Nearest Hurricane, L2001, was an A Flight aircraft, which was eventually lost when Sergeant Pascoe was killed in a take-off crash at Hatfield, June 19th, 1940. The triple-hose petrol bowser could feed three aircraft at the same time—a 'bonus' for quick turn-round between patrols throughout the Battle of Britain.

Tribute
TOM GLEAVE

Tom Gleave, commander of 253 Squadron, took off from Biggin Hill on August 31st, 1940 at the head of seven Hurricanes to tackle an approaching bomber formation, and after plunging into a huge gaggle of Junkers 88 bombers and damaging two, was on the receiving end of a crippling burst of cannon fire. His Hurricane, P3115, erupted in flames and its starboard wing ripped off. Grievously burned, Gleave managed to take to his parachute and came to earth just east of his own airfield. His injuries led to him becoming one of the first plastic surgery patients of the legendary Archibald McIndoe—the 'Guinea Pigs'—and subsequently he returned to active service and eventually retired as a Group Captain.

At the time of the Battle of Britain the Hurricane was one of the finest fighters in the world. She was not the fastest, being some 30mph slower than the Spitfire and 33mph or so slower than the Messer-schmitt Bf 109E-3. And above 20,000 feet her performance fell away rapidly. But below that height she was incredibly manoeuvrable, much more than the Spit-fire and outstandingly against the Me 109. By contemporary standards, visibility from her cockpit was excellent, and she provided a superb gun platform. Immensely strong, she could absorb enormous punishment. I once saw a Hurricane being literally chewed up by the guns and cannons of an Me 109 from the cockpit aft, yet when I landed back at base that same Hurricane was already down safely and parked on the tarmac, looking like a half-devoured herring! The Hurricane was also easy to maintain, her serviceability being little short of remarkable. Equally important, she was comparatively easy to repair because of her simple construction as opposed to that of the Spitfire and Me 109 which, with their stressed skins, were in some ways 'delicate', to say the least. The Hurricane had a wide, generous and robust

Readiness. Pilots of 32 Squadron relaxing between sorties at Hawkinge forward airfield, July 31st, 1940. In background, Hurricane P3522, GZ-V, with a parachute harness ready for quick donning on its tailplane.

undercarriage capable of withstanding very rough treatment—a boon in operational service, training units and at night. On the other hand the Spitfire and Me 109 had delicate undercarriages for which a heavy price in each case was paid in training, and even in squadron service, and it appears that on this account neither aircraft instilled much confidence in inexperienced pilots at night, apart from the other hazards of night flying.

To fly the Hurricane was sheer pleasure. She had no vices, other than the stall, from which even her feathered friends were not immune. She answered every call made on her with a will, sharing with the Spitfire the joy of having the impeccably-mannered Rolls-Royce Merlin to attend to her every whim. She took off without any marked swinging tantrum from which other, less well-bred types suffered. She was unbelievably stable, and in cloud or at night, when rudder and elevator tabs were properly adjusted, she would settle down into a 'rut' of her own making whether going up or down. And at no time was this virtue more precious than when taking off on a pitch-dark night and climbing into a coal-black void. Nor above all when coming in to land in bad weather or at night. Then, with flaps and undercarriage down, tabs adjusted, and at half-throttle, she would float down serenely until the airfield, or at night, the faint glow of the Glim lights or goose-neck flares came into view. A gentle levelling out would cause her to sink until the vibration of her rumbling wheels told the pilot to close the throttle.

In a dogfight the Hurricane could almost turn on her tail as her guns spat tracer, lead and incendiary at anything that dared try to join the circle. In pursuit she could cut the corners, and only when the superior climb or dive of the Me 109 took it out of danger had she to look for other 'game'. When making her own getaway, she took without complaint the quickest of flick-rolls and U-turns, and 'standing on the rudder bar' held no terrors for her or her pilot. Though she played a great part in fighter-versus-fighter events, she perhaps found her most profitable role in the Battle of Britain in attacking enemy bomber formations and their close escorts —close-knit mêlées ensuing in which her magnificent manoeuvrability and control paid handsome dividends. Meanwhile the Spitfires held at bay and fought the massive enemy fighter top covers above. In this way, with the graceful Spitfire holding the ring and the Hurricane, like the Amazon she was, clobbering everything that wore a swastika within it, those two great fighters were complementary to each other. It was a lethal partnership that has never been excelled and, perhaps, never will be. In it the wonderful Hurricane was at least an equal partner. A true 'fighting lady', if ever there was one.

Below left: Before the storm. B Flight pilots of 17 Squadron, Debden, July 1940. From left: Fg Off H. A.C. Bird-Wilson, Plt Off Leeming (killed in action, August 25th, 1940), Sgt D. A. Sewell, Sqn Ldr C. W. Williams (OC), killed in action, August 25th, 1940, Plt Off D. H. Wissler (killed in action, November 11th, 1940) and Plt Off J. K. Ross (killed in action after Battle of Britain).

Readiness. Squadron Leader E. A. McNab, commander of No 1 Canadian Squadron, seated in his Hurricane at Northolt on September 12th, 1940.

First Flight
GRAHAM LEGGETT

September 5th, 1940. E Flight dispersal, 5 OTU, Aston Down. With mounting excitement I walk out to the Hurricane and settle into the familiar cockpit. Familiar because although I am about to fly a Hurricane for the first time, as a student at Hawker Aircraft I helped assemble the first production machines. Ever since Cyril Wells and Ben Hogbin positioned the jigs and skilfully built the basic airframe, the Hurricane had been 'my' aeroplane. At Brooklands the pro-

Scramble. 56 Squadron gets away from North Weald aerodrome.

totype was piling up the hours and, in no time it seemed, the first squadron, 111, was formed at Northolt. Knowing the nuts and bolts was to help me save a machine later, but for the moment I 'flew' deadly combat within the Erection Shop walls. Bill Clarke once prised me from the cockpit, muttering 'Hop out now and let Mr Sopwith (T.O.M.) have a go.' But now it is for real. 173 hours in Tiger Moths and Miles Masters are to be put to the test in a powerful machine of which no trainer version exists.

Cockpit check—thumbs up—switches on—press the starter button. A few turns of the two-bladed airscrew, blue-grey smoke puffs from the exhausts and the Merlin roars into life. Jinking to improve forward vision on differential brakes proves tricky and I suspect the pilot of an approaching Blenheim expressed an opinion

About to taxy. Hurricane P3522, GZ-V of 32 Squadron prepares to take off from Hawkinge, July 31st, 1940.

before I gave him a spot on which to land. At take-off power the Hurricane needs a fair bit of right rudder, then, almost unexpectedly, she leaps eagerly off the grass and flies. Unconsciously moving the stick when reaching for the undercarriage lever, I immediately have to pick up the nose and port wing—God! these controls are sensitive! But what a beautiful aeroplane—instant obedience to the controls, superb view, and what power. So much in fact that one's leg aches holding her in a prolonged climb. Levelling out at 10,000 feet, I check position and fuel and apply aileron. Easing back the stick the nose follows the horizon effortlessly—in fact, she almost flies herself and the rudder seems superfluous. More bank, now rudder to steady the nose, back with the stick, and she's tearing round vertically in the opposite direction. For the next 15 minutes I have the time of my life. Diving and climbing turns, rolling, stalling—the Hurricane flies like the thoroughbred bird she truly is. There's much to learn, but already I know the Hurricane's secret—superb manoeuvrability, the quality above all others that is to make her a legend.

Now it's time to try a landing, without the help of an instructor. R/T reception on the novel TR9 is poor, though I'm later to be astonished by the efficiency of VHF. Once in the circuit things happen rather quickly, but the Hurricane's lack of vices and ready response at low speed brought her cleanly to touch-down and she sat down quite daintily. A couple more circuits and I'm taxying in, feeling pretty pleased with myself, and more than pleased with this wonderful aeroplane that has become the focal point of my young being.

Widge
IAN GLEED

Ian 'Widge' Gleed, a pre-1939 pilot who flew Gloster Gauntlets with 46 Squadron, first saw action with 87 Squadron in France during the May 1940 German *Blitzkrieg* offensive. He remained with 87 for nearly two years of operational flying, rising to command of the squadron and gaining nearly 20 victories—all on Hurricanes. Promoted to Wing Commander, he subsequently commanded a fighter Wing in North Africa and was killed in action on April 16th, 1943, having received a DSO, DFC and two foreign gallantry awards for his prowess and inspired leadership. The following account, in his own words, describes intimately his thoughts and actions during just one massive combat of the Battle of Britain struggle, specifically August 25th, 1940.

I glance back at the 'drome. Twelve dots are climbing behind us. Lucky devils, 213 Squadron: they are after the bombers again. It's a glorious day. The sun beats down on us. The sea looks most inviting. Hope I don't have to bathe just yet. At last we are slowly catching B Flight up. I glance at the instrument panel. Everything looks normal; radiator temperature on the high side, nothing to worry about, as it's a hell of a hot day. It seems hard to realise that over the sea masses of Jerry aircraft are flying, aiming to drop their bombs on the peaceful-looking countryside that lies beneath. Up, up. My two wing men are crouching forward in their cockpits, their hoods open. I slide mine open: it's too damned stuffy with it shut. My mouth feels hellishly dry; there is a strong sinking feeling in my breast. Thank God a doctor isn't listening to my heart. It's absolutely banging away. Turn on the oxygen a bit more. We are now at 20,000. It is cooler now, so I slam the hood shut. It's a hell of a long way to fall. Once more the sun shines from the sea, its reflection off the surface makes it nearly impossible to look in that direction. Yet that direction is where the Hun is coming from. At last, 22,000 feet. We all throttle back and close up. I climb to 26,000, level out. On the R/T rather faintly comes, 'bandits now south-west of Portland Bill.' We are in perfect position to intercept them.

Below us, like a model, lies Portland Harbour. A sunken ship standing in shallow waters, half submerged, looks like a microscopic model. Back with the hood. I strain my eyes peering at the blue sky. Nothing yet. Far below us another squadron is weaving; just below me B Flight is weaving violently. Dickie and 'Dinkie' criss-cross behind my tail. I peer forward, heading out to sea.

'Tally-ho.' 'Christ, there they are.' A weaving, darting mass of dots gradually drift toward us, looking like a cloud of midges on a summer evening. 'Hell! was I born to die today?' 'Line astern, line astern, go.'

Dickie and 'Dinkie' swing under my tail. The Jerries seem miles above us; lines of smaller dots show where the 109s are ready to pounce. Beneath them, about our height, circles of 110s turn, chasing each others' tails, moving as a mass slowly towards us. Far below, the bombers are in tight formation. Somehow they look like tin soldiers. 'Steady; don't attack too soon.' Johnny and B Flight have dived, heading for the bombers; they have swung into line astern and now swing into echelon. The 110s continue circling. They seem to make no attempt to dive. 'Here goes'. I dive at the nearest circle of 110s. 'Christ! look out.'

A glance behind shows 109s literally falling out of the sky, on top of us. Messerschmitts. I bank into a steep turn. Now we are in a defensive circle, the 109s overshoot us and climb steeply. Now's our chance. I straighten out and go for the closest 110. 'You silly b . . . . . .!' He turns away from me. I turn the firing button on to Fire; at exactly 250 yards I give him a quick burst. White puffs are flashing past the cockpit. Another burst. 'Got him!' A terrific burst of fire from his starboard engine, a black dot and a puff of white as the pilot's parachute opens. I bank into a steep left-hand turn and watch for a split second the burning 110 going vertically downwards. The parachutist is surrounded by 'planes, darting here and there. 'Thank God! got one of them. Now for another'. Below me another circle of nine 110s are firing at a solitary Hurricane which is turning inside them. I shove the nose down, sights on the last one, thumb the firing button. 'Oh, what a lovely deflection shot! Got him!' White smoke pours from one engine, more white vapour from his wings; his wings glint as he rolls on his back. Another burst. 'Hell, look out!' A large chunk of something flashes by my wings; as I glance behind I see tracer flash by my tail.

A 109 is just about on my tail; the stick comes back in my tummy, and everything goes away. Now an aileron turn downwards, down. 'That was a near one.' I miss a 110 by inches—down; at 400mph on the clock. The controls are solid. Nothing seems to be behind me. I wind gently on the trimming wheel, straighten out and start a steep climb. What seems miles above me the Jerries still whirl. I can't see any friendly 'planes at all. 'Hell! where am I?

About ten miles off the coast. Hurrah, they're going home.' I turn for the shore, weaving fiercely. Over to the west the bombers are haring back in twos and threes. Two Hurricanes appear to be chasing them. I can catch them easily. 'Here goes. There's one. Looks like an 88. That will do me nicely.' The escort fighters still seem a long way above me. I am gaining fast—about 400 yards now. 'Damn, the 'Hurricanes' have black crosses on them—109s; coming straight for me, head-on attack. Right, you bastards! I'll give you hell before you get me.' Sights on, I thumb the button. A stream of tracer tears over my head. 'Blast! missed him. Now come on number two.' He heads straight for me. I yank back on the stick, kick on rudder and turn down on to the 109. 'That shook you up, didn't it'. Sights on. Brrrrrrrrrrrrrrrr, brrrrrrrrrr. mmmmmmmmm. A streak of black comes from his engine, a stream of tracers flashes past my nose. 'God, I must get out of this.' Another aileron turn. 'Down, down, down. Pull out now, or you'll be in the drink.' The coast is nearly out of sight. 'Oh God, don't let them get me.' I screw round in the cockpit. Nothing is in sight. I scream along just above the water. I glance at the rev counter. I'm so deaf that I'm not sure that the motor is going. It looks all right. I hurtle past many patches of oil. At last the cliffs loom up. I turn westwards. Several patches of fluorescence show where pilots are in the water. Motorboats are chugging towards them. The sea is dead calm, glassy. 'I'm still alive.'

Scramble. A Vic of three Hurricanes from 312 (Czech) Squadron fly over V6935, Speke, 1940.

Battle over London

J. SAMPLE

On September 15th, 1940, the true climax of the Battle of Britain was reached. On that Sunday RAF Fighter Command achieved final and unequivocal superiority over the assaulting Luftwaffe formations over southern England. Appropriately, it is this date which annually commemorates the Battle throughout the British Commonwealth. The following first-hand account was by the late Squadron Leader J. Sample, DFC, on that date commander of 504 Squadron. The sergeant pilot mentioned, who landed by parachute in a Chelsea garden, was R. T. Holmes, whose victim crashed in the forecourt of Victoria rail station, London.

At lunchtime on Sunday, my squadron was somewhere south of the Thames estuary behind several other squadrons of Hurricanes and Spitfires. The German bombers were three or four miles away when we first spotted them. We were at 17,000 feet and they were at about 19,000 feet. Their fighter escort was scattered around. The bombers were coming in towards London from the south-east, and at first we could not tell how many there were. We opened our throttles and started to climb towards them, aiming for a point well ahead, where we expected to contact them at their own height. As we converged on them I saw there were about 20 of them, and it looked as though it were going to be a nice party, for the other squadrons of Hurricanes and Spitfires also turned to join in. By the time we reached a position near the bombers we were over London—central London I should say. We had gained a little height on them too, so when I gave the order to attack we were able to dive on them from their right.

Each of us selected his own target. Our first attack broke them up pretty nicely. The Dornier I attacked with a burst

lasting several seconds began to turn left away from his friends. I gave him five seconds and he went away with white smoke streaming behind him. As I broke away and started to make a steep climbing turn I looked over the side. I recognised the river immediately below me through a hole in the clouds. I saw the bends in the river, and the bridges, and idly wondered where I was. I didn't recognise it immediately, and then I saw Kennington Oval. I saw the covered stands round the Oval, and I thought to myself; 'That is where they play cricket'. It's queer how, in the middle of a battle, one can see something on the ground and think of something entirely different from the immediate job in hand. I remember I had a flashing thought—a sort of mental picture—of a big man with a beard, but at that moment I did not think of the name of W. G. Grace. It was just a swift, passing thought as I climbed back to the fight.

I found myself very soon below another Dornier which had white smoke coming from it. It was being attacked by two Hurricanes and a Spitfire, and it was travelling north and turning slightly to the right. As I could not see anything else to attack at that moment, I went to join in. I climbed up above him and did a diving attack on him. Coming in to attack I noticed what appeared to be a red light shining in the rear gunner's cockpit, but when I got closer I realised I was looking right through the gunner's cockpit into the pilot's and observer's cockpit beyond. The

Top right: 'His starboard engine exploded'—a Heinkel III at the receiving end of an eight-gun burst of machine gun fire.

Centre right: 'He streamed smoke and fell straight down'—a Junkers 88 about to die.

Centre left: Vapour trails—a constant scene in the skies of England during the summer of 1940, recalling Stephen Spender's lines: ". . . and left the vivid air signed with their honour".

Far right: 'Tally-Ho'. A Heinkel III sits dead-centre of the gun ring.

Right: Climbing to battle. 85 Squadron's Hurricanes, led by Squadron Leader Peter Townsend, DFC, in tight formation above a cloud carpet in the late summer of 1940. Nearest aircraft is V6611.

red light was fire. I gave it a quick burst and as I passed him on the right I looked in through the big glass nose of the Dornier It was like a furnace inside. He began to go down, and we watched. In a few seconds the tail came off, and the bomber did a forward somersault and then went into a spin. After he had done two turns in his spin his wings broke off outboard of the engines, so that all that was left as the blazing aircraft fell was half a fuselage and the wing roots with the engines on the end of them. This dived straight down, just past the edge of a cloud, and then the cloud got in the way and I could see no more of him. The battle was over by then. I couldn't see anything else to shoot at, so I flew home. Our squadron's score was five certainties—including one by a sergeant pilot, who landed by parachute in a Chelsea garden.

An hour later we were in the air again, meeting more bombers and fighters coming in. We got three more—our squadron, I mean. I started to chase one Dornier which was flying through the tops of the clouds. Did you ever see that film *Hell's Angels*? You'll remember how the Zeppelin came so slowly out of the cloud. Well, this Dornier reminded me of that. I attacked him four times altogether. When he first appeared through the cloud—you know how clouds go up and down like foam on water—I fired at him from the left, swung over to the right, turned in towards another hollow in the cloud, where I expected him to reappear, and fired at him

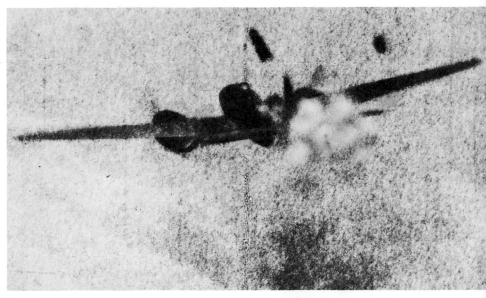

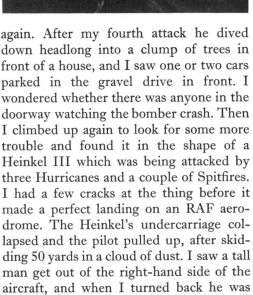

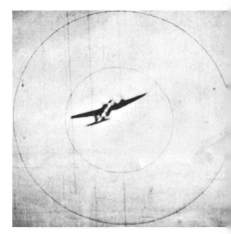

again. After my fourth attack he dived down headlong into a clump of trees in front of a house, and I saw one or two cars parked in the gravel drive in front. I wondered whether there was anyone in the doorway watching the bomber crash. Then I climbed up again to look for some more trouble and found it in the shape of a Heinkel III which was being attacked by three Hurricanes and a couple of Spitfires. I had a few cracks at the thing before it made a perfect landing on an RAF aerodrome. The Heinkel's undercarriage collapsed and the pilot pulled up, after skidding 50 yards in a cloud of dust. I saw a tall man get out of the right-hand side of the aircraft, and when I turned back he was helping a small man across the aerodrome towards a hangar.

Combat Report-1
J. H. LACEY

James H. Lacey, 'Ginger' to all who knew him, was a sergeant pilot at the opening of the Battle of Britain, serving with 501 Squadron, AAF, with which unit he had already been 'blooded' in combat in France during the May 1940 *Blitzkrieg*. By the end of the Battle of Britain he had been credited with at least 16 victories in the air. On September 2nd Lacey was at the head of a section of Hurricanes patrolling over the Ashford Kent area just after 8am. He sighted some 50 Dornier 215 bombers, escorted by about another 50 Messerschmitt 109s. In his own words:

I was leading Yellow Section of A Flight, when No 501 Squadron attacked the Me 109s escorting about 30 Do 215s . . . three Me 109s had climbed above the Flight, and to prevent them diving on to the squadron from behind, I also climbed and attacked them. I was able to get in a good burst of about five seconds at a red-cowled 109, but the EA immediately turned, and I observed no damage. I followed it round in the turn, I was unable to bring my guns to bear, but after about 30 seconds of circling, the Me 109 pilot jumped out and did a delayed drop of about 5,000 feet, before opening his parachute. Most of the other Me 109s were engaged, so I dived out of the dog-fight and attacked No 5 in the last formation of Do 215s . . . Almost as soon as I opened fire, the Do 215 broke out of formation, and turned SE with smoke issuing from its starboard engine . . . I continued to fire until my ammunition was exhausted, when I broke away to the side, and then formated on it about quarter of a mile away, to the right, to observe results. The enemy aircraft lost height rapidly, until it reached 5,000 feet, which seemed to be its absolute ceiling on one engine, and then proceeded out to sea towards France, losing height very slowly . . . I then returned to base and landed.

Below: Return from combat. A 32 Squadron Hurricane lets down at Biggin Hill, August 15th, 1940; whilst two companions behind circle into finals.

Above: Ammunition exhausted, fuel low, a Hurricane of 17 Squadron piloted by Flight Lieutenant W. J. Harper, rolls towards its dispersal at Debden, July 1940, assisted by two of the faithful groundcrews.

Far left: Pilot Officer A. G. Lewis, DFC climbs out of his 85 Squadron Hurricane, VY-R, at Croydon, September 1940. A South African, Lewis fought in France with 504 and 85 Squadrons gaining nine victories. In September 1940 he joined 249 Squadron and added a further nine victories to his tally. He eventually commanded 261 Squadron in Iraq and Ceylon and ended the war with a credited score of 21 at least.

Group Captain (later Air Vice-Marshal) Stanley F. Vincent was commander of RAF Northolt during the high summer of 1940. A fighter pilot of repute during the 1914–18 air war, Vincent was 43 years old —possibly the oldest of the 'Few'—when, typically, he took off alone on September 15th seeking the Luftwaffe.

When at 19,000 feet near Biggin Hill I saw a large formation of enemy bombers, escorted by fighters, in the south-east, and when flying towards it saw a formation of 18 Do 215s approaching from the south, escorted by 20 Me 109s. The bombers were in Vics of three sections in line astern— fighters 2–3,000 feet above and in no apparent formation. There were no other British fighters in sight, so I made a head-on attack on the first section of bombers, opening at 600 yards and closing to 200 yards. I saw the De Wilde (incendiary) ammunition hit the EA. On breaking away I noticed that five of the bombers were continuing northwards together with apparently all the fighters, whilst 13 of the bombers had turned right round and were proceeding due south. I made further attacks on the retreating bombers, each attack from climbing beam, and I could see the De Wilde ammunition hitting in each attack. In one instance I could see De Wilde hit the main part of the fuselage and the wing group. One Dornier left the formation and lost height. With no ammunition left I could not finish it off. I last saw the bomber at 3,000 feet dropping slowly and still travelling south.

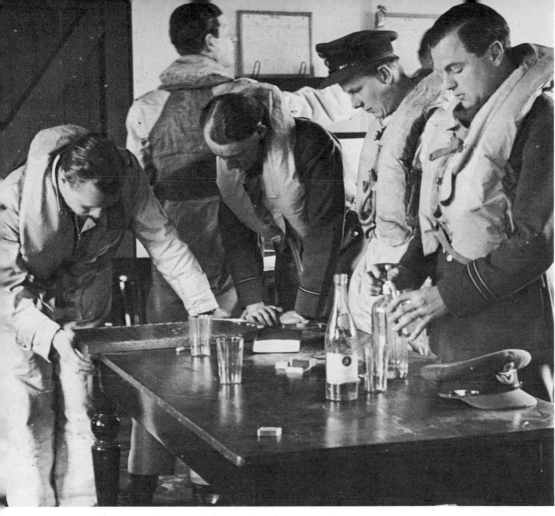

Far left: Re-arm, re-fuel, stand by. Pilots of 061 Squadron, AAF at Tangmere 1940 stretch their legs while waiting for the ground crews to replenish their aircraft. Pilot at left is Max Aitken. Note the flat-loader home-made trolley in front of Aitken, used for transporting ammunition.

Far left: Turn-round. The 'erks' (ground crews) clamber over the aircraft to prepare it for its next sortie. At the height of the battle turn-round time on some fighter squadrons reached an all-time 'low' of four minutes in practised hands.

Above: Pause for a few moment's relaxation. 601 Squadron pilots in the Readiness hut, Tangmere. Round the table, from left: Flight Lieutenant W. H. 'Willy' Rhodes-Moorhouse, DFC (killed in action, September 6th, 1940), Charles Lee Steer, Pilot Officer R. S. 'Dick' Demetriadi (killed in action, August 11th, 1940) and Flight Lieutenant Max Aitken (now Sir Max Aitken, Bart, DSO, DFC).

Left: War Trophy. 17 Squadron pilots displaying the fin of a Junkers 88, the destruction of which was shared between them, August 1940, From left: Sqn Ldr C. W. Williams, Plt Off J. K. Ross and Fg Off C. A. H. Bird-Wilson. The chalked figure '78' referred to the squadron's claimed total victories as at August 21st, 1940.

Hurricane VC
J.B. NICOLSON

James Brindley Nicolson was unique as a fighter pilot in that he was the only man to gain the award of a Victoria Cross for fighter operations during the 1939–45 war. Originally joining the RAF in December 1936, he was trained as a pilot and joined 72 Squadron, with which unit he was still serving after the outbreak of war. In May 1940 he was posted to 249 Squadron, and on August 16th, 1940, was acting A Flight commander when he engaged in his first air combat. It was this combat which is described here, in his own words, and which led to the VC award. The severe burn injuries he received that day kept him away from operational flying for a year, and in October 1942, as a Wing Commander, he was posted to the Far East for a staff job at Alipore, Calcutta. On August 4th, 1943, Nicolson finally got his wish for active operations when he was appointed CO of 27 Squadron, flying Beaufighters and Mosquitos against the Japanese. His tour with 27 resulted in the award of a DFC. On May 2nd, 1945, Nicolson was a 'passenger' in a Liberator bomber of 355 Squadron raiding Japanese targets. The bomber crashed in the sea, with only two survivors—Nicolson was not one of these. The following account of his VC combat was published shortly after his award was announced. For propaganda purposes it omits the fact that Nicolson received a further injury during his parachute descent—a bullet in the buttock fired by an over-zealous Royal Artillery gunner . . .

Hurricane VC—Flt Lt James Brindley Nicolson of 249 Squadron who, for his first combat sortie on August 16th, was later awarded a Victoria Cross. In 1945, as Wing Commander, VC, DFC, Nicolson failed to return from a bombing sortie.

That day was a glorious day. The sun was shining from a cloudless sky and there was hardly a breath of wind anywhere. Our squadron was going towards Southampton on patrol at 15,000 feet when I saw three Junkers 88 bombers about four miles away flying across our bows. I reported this to our squadron leader and he replied, 'Go after them with your section'. So I led my section of aircraft round towards the bombers. We chased hard after them, but when we were about a mile behind we saw the 88s fly straight into a squadron of Spitfires. I used to fly a Spitfire myself and I guessed it was curtains for the three Junkers. I was right and they were all shot down in quick time, with no pickings for us. I must confess I was very disappointed, for I had never fired at a German in my life and was longing to have a crack at them. So we swung round again and started to climb up to 18,000 feet over Southampton, to rejoin our squadron. I was still a long way from the squadron when suddenly, very close in rapid succession, I heard four big bangs. They were the loudest noises I had ever heard, and they had been made by four cannon shells from a Messer-schmitt 110 hitting my machine.

The first shell tore through the hood over my cockpit and sent splinters into my left eye. One splinter, I discovered later, nearly severed my eyelid. I couldn't see through that eye for blood. The second cannon shell struck my spare petrol tank and set it on fire. The third shell crashed into the cockpit and tore off my right trouser leg. The fourth shell struck the back of my left shoe and made quite a mess of my left foot. But I didn't know anything about that, either, until later. Anyway, the effect of these four shells was to make me dive away to the right to avoid further shells. Then I started cursing myself for my carelessness. What a fool I had been, I thought, what a fool! I was just thinking of jumping out when suddenly a Messerschmitt 110 whizzed under me and got right in my gunsights. Fortunately, no damage had been done to my windscreens or sights and when I was chasing the Junkers I had switched everything on. So everything was set for a fight. I pressed the gun button, for the Messerschmitt was in nice range; I plugged him the first time and I could see my tracer

Section Leader. Flight Lieutenant Ian 'Widge' Gleed, DFC in Hurricane P2798, LK-A, *Figaro* leading a section of 87 Squadron's aircraft from Exeter to Bibury, September 1940. This Hurricane fought (with 87) through the battles of France and Britain, 1940, and Ian Gleed was almost its only pilot during that period, gaining nearly 20 victories in this machine.

Freedom Fighters. 310 Czech Squadron at Duxford, September 1st, 1940. The unit was formed initially on July 10th, 1940 and had its first combat on August 26th. The seated pilot in RAF uniform (centre) is an Englishman, Flight Lieutenant J. Jefferies, DFC, a Flight commander of the original unit. In background, Hurricane P3143, NN-D.

Right: Freedom fighters. No 303 Polish Squadron's aircraft at Northolt in September 1940. Each aircraft carried the Polish insignia 'Kosciuszko' just aft of the cockpit. 303 first formed on August 2nd, 1940; and a total of 154 Polish pilots fought in the Battle of Britain, 30 of these being killed in action.

Below right: Two Vics of well-worn Hurricanes of 245 Squadron from Aldergrove, Northern Ireland, late 1940. Nearest aircraft is P3762, DX-F.

bullets entering the German machine. He was going like mad, twisting and turning as he tried to get away from my fire. So I pushed the throttle wide open. Both of us must have been doing about 400mph as we went down together in a dive. First he turned left, then right, then left and right again. He did three turns to the right and finally a fourth turn to the left. I remember shouting out loud to him when I first saw him, 'I'll teach you some manners', and I shouted other things as well. I knew I was getting him nearly all the time I was firing.

By this time it was pretty hot inside my machine from the burst petrol tank. I couldn't see much flame, but I reckon it was there all right. I remember looking once at my left hand which was keeping the throttle open. It seemed to be in the fire itself and I could see the skin peeling off it. Yet I had little pain. Unconsciously too, I had drawn my feet up under my parachute on the seat, to escape the heat I suppose. Well, I gave the German all I had, and the last I saw of him was when he was going down, with his right wing lower than the left wing. I gave him a parting burst and as he had disappeared, started thinking about saving myself. I decided it was about time I left the aircraft and baled out, so I immediately jumped up from my seat. But first of all I hit my head against the framework of the hood, which was all that was left. I cursed myself for a fool, pulled the hood back (wasn't I relieved when it slid back beautifully and jumped up again. Once again I bounced back into my seat, for I had forgotten to undo the straps holding me in. One of them snapped and so I only had to undo one. Then I left the machine.

I suppose I was about 12–15,000 feet when I baled out. Immediately I started somersaulting downwards and after a few turns like that I found myself diving head first for the ground. After a second or two of this, I decided to pull the rip-cord. The result was that I immediately straightened out and began to float down. Then an aircraft—a Messerschmitt I think—came tearing past me. I decided to pretend I was dead, and hung limply by the parachute straps. The Messerschmitt came back once, and I kept my eyes closed, but I didn't get the bullets I was half-expecting. I don't know if he fired at me; the main thing is that I wasn't hit.

While I was coming down like that, I had a good look at myself. I could see the bones of my left hand showing through the knuckles. Then for the first time I discovered I'd been wounded in the foot. Blood was oozing out of the lace holes of my left boot. My right hand was pretty badly burned too. So I hung down a bit longer and then decided to try my limbs, just to see if they would work—thank goodness, they did. I still had my oxygen mask over my face, but my hands were in too bad a state to take it off. I tried to, but I couldn't manage it. I found too that I had lost one trouser leg and the other was badly torn and my tunic was just like a lot of torn rags, so I wasn't looking very smart. Then, after a bit more of this dangling down business, I began to ache all over and my hands and leg began to hurt a lot.

When I got lower I saw I was in danger of coming down in the sea. I knew I didn't stand an earthly if I did, because I wouldn't have been able to swim a stroke with my hands like that. So I wriggled about a bit and managed to float inland. Then I saw a high tension cable below me and thought it would finish me if I hit that. So I wriggled a bit more and aimed at a nice open field. When I was about 100 feet from the ground I saw a cyclist and heard him ring his bell. I was surprised to hear the bicycle bell and realised that I had been coming down in absolute silence. I bellowed at the cyclist, but I don't suppose he heard me. Finally, I touched down in the field and fell over. Fortunately it was a still day. My parachute just floated down and stayed down without dragging me along, as they sometimes do. I had a piece of good news almost immediately. One of the people who came along and who had watched the combat, said they had seen the Messerschmitt 110 dive straight into the sea.

First Fights
GRAHAM LEGGETT

To go into battle is the most overwhelmingly exciting event any 19 year old can experience. To do so at the controls of a Hurricane has left indelible images upon the mind's eye of those who had that unique privilege. The heat of the Scramble, the chase across a field of balloons supporting a silvery Thames, the thrust above London's blanketing murk. The misty shapes of adjacent aircraft swirling through cloud and then, suddenly, the sheer beauty of a squadron of Hurricanes bursting through into the sunshine above. Through the earphones a controlling voice plotting 'bandits', AA puffs growing into a dark cloud against the blue. Higher yet, hoods are snapped shut, radiator shutters adjusted, oxygen masks wheezing loudly. Faint wisps streaming from exhausts, thickening into white trails. Someone reports 'aircraft above' as loosely connected white trails pass overhead, curving as they work towards the sun. Stepped down in threes line astern, 12 Hurricanes swing round, gun buttons and sights are set, an urgent voice warns 'Snappers astern'. Tracer snaking past the cockpit, blunt yellow noses on slender bodies flashing past, iron crosses on straight, squared wings flitting so briefly through gunsights, blue bellies arcing into the void.

At this stage of the Battle of Britain (October), Luftwaffe tactics consisted of high-flying formations of Bf 109s attacking London with 550lb bombs. On October 25th, 46 Squadron was scrambled from breakfast in the Mess, only in time to see 20 of these fighter/bombers far above, heading home. But later in the day we met another 20 head-on, and at least had the pleasure of seeing them jettison their bombs as they turned tail and dived back to France. If only we had more height. Clearly the Hurricane was at its best around 15,000 feet, but without wishing to swap mounts, one had to envy the Spitfire's ability to tackle the 109s from higher altitude. Against massed bomber formations the Hurricane had proved herself a battle-winner; against current Luftwaffe tactics she would be more effective with extra power. Nevertheless Hurricane pilots gave as good as they got and, as was to happen repeatedly, the Germans, confidence ebbing, failed to press home their advantage.

As October 1940 drew to a close our squadron (46) was being jumped almost daily. On the 29th, in Hurricane V7610, I was scrambled to 15,000 feet over base (Stapleford Tawney). As 'Pip Squeak' aircraft, I provided our IFF radar blip and, therefore, missed some of the R/T transmissions. But I did hear our 'Arse-end Charlie' shout 'Snappers' and, even as we broke, saw one of our formation plunge away in flames. As I completed a 360 degrees vertical turn, a 109 came towards me from slightly below with a Hurricane reaching for its tail. The 109 pulled up in a steep climbing turn to port and I followed. Almost at once he was in my sights,

87 Squadron formation, September 1940. Pilots were Ian Gleed (aircraft 'A'), Ken Tait (E), Sgt F. Howell (Z) and Francois de Spirlet (T).

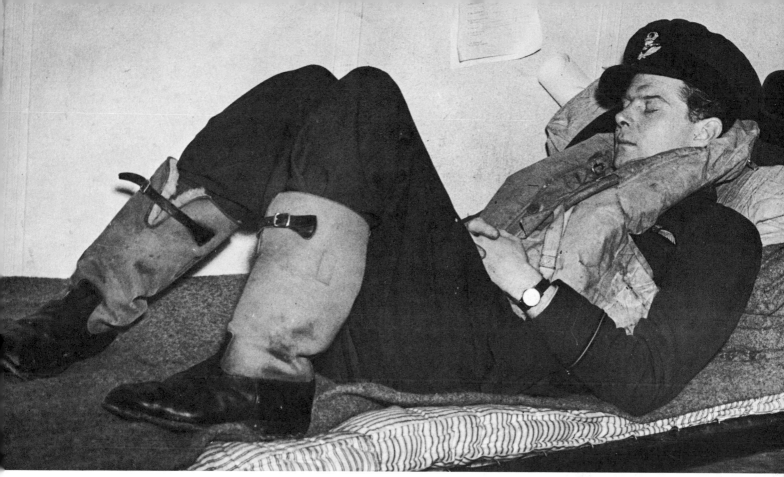

climbing steeply. Jabbing my thumb on the button I fired two long bursts from fully astern, breaking away sharply as another 109 attacked from above. It pulled up again and, with everyone else, disappeared. Just how the sky empties itself, when only moments before it had been full of aircraft, was very mysterious. Eventually I found another Hurricane and together we returned to base. At the subsequent post-mortem I learned that 'my' 109's pilot had baled out just as I broke away.

Early in November 1940 we learned that Italian aircraft were operating in south-east England. November 11th was indeed a day to remember. In Hurricane V7604 I was in a formation of 12 patrolling a convoy off Harwich, below cloud. Soon we were vectored on to 40-plus bandits at 12,000 feet. Then, through a break in the cloud, we beheld a lovely sight! A dozen plump twin-engined bombers some 5,000 feet above. Already Hurricanes of 257 Squadron were tearing into them and as we clawed up underneath the bombers, jettisoned bombs plunged past our wing tips. Now the bombers were falling away as well and odd bits of wreckage fluttered down. One bomber dived away to star-

board and I recognised it as a Fiat BR20— the Regia Aeronautica had come to 'finish off' Britain! I turned in on a quarter attack and even as I pressed the gun button, a door flew open and the crew started diving out. The remaining Italians pressed on towards Orfordness—at last I had bombers to shoot at. After some clumsy attacks on various targets I singled out a BR20 on the extreme left for close attention. My first attack was good and he let his bombs go in the sea. Closing in again I fired a long, steady burst—and ran out of ammunition! My quarry was now diving inland and there was nothing else to do but escort him down. Over my shoulder I observed only two remaining bombers and what looked like a cloud of midges darting all over the sky. This turned out to be the fighter escort, some 40 Fiat CR42 biplanes, which had mislaid the bombers somewhere over the North Sea. Some of the Hurricanes had ammunition to knock down a few, and one hapless CR42 pilot lost his head to a Hurricane's airscrew. After a few minutes my BR20 nosed towards a large field and came to a standstill in a fir plantation.

A photo which, in a way, sums up the effort made by RAF fighter pilots during the desperate struggle in the air in 1940. Flying Officer W. P. Clyde of 601 Squadron AAF snatches a brief sleep between sorties. The high-key tension of constant fighting during the battle swiftly exhausted pilots, and sleep was taken anywhere, anytime it was possible.

Russian Episode
J.K.ROSS DIARY

Gloster-built Hurricane IIb,
Z5252, piloted by a Russian
General, prepares for take-
off from Vaenga airstrip,
near Murmansk. To assist
performance, this machine
was fitted with only eight
machine guns.

It is not generally recognised just how massive was the aid, in terms of material and machines, given to the USSR by the Allies during 1941–45. This assistance was particularly evident in the context of the Hurricane. Altogether a total of nearly 3,000 Hurricanes were supplied to Russia —just under 20 per cent of all Hurricanes built. When Germany opened hostilities against Russia on June 22nd, 1941, the British Prime Minister, Winston Churchill, immediately pledged utmost support to the new ally, firstly in the form of large shipping convoys of vital war materials round the North Cape and into Russian ports at Murmansk, Arkhangel'sk and Petsamo. To protect these convoys, two new RAF squadrons, 81 and 134, were formed as 151 Wing RAF in August 1941. Equipped with Hurricane IIBs, these were shipped to Vaenga airfield, some 20 miles from Murmansk, and there provided

operational example and instruction to the Red Air Force. One of the Flight commanders of 134 Squadron was the late J. K. Ross, a veteran of the Battle of Britain in which he had served with 17 Squadron, gained four certain victories and three probables, and was later awarded a DFC. His log book entries for the time he served in Russia, which were virtually a day-to-day diary account, are reproduced here verbatim—a unique document, and a tribute to a truly courageous man.

Formation of No. 151 Wing
On July 29th, one complete Flight of 17 Squadron detached and sent to Leconfield to form No 134 Squadron of 151 Wing. Flight consisted of—CO, S/Ldr A. G, Miller, Self, P/Os Cameron, Furneaux, Wollaston, Sheldon and Sgts Barnes. Clark, Campbell & Gould. Flight personnel were mostly from B Flight, 17

Centre: Hurricanes of 134 Squadron preparing for a sortie over the fighting zone. In foreground, Z5236, GO-31, and behind, Z5159, GV-33. The sub-zero air temperatures, combined with inferior petrol (of Russian origin) combined to give much trouble with the Hurricanes' engines.

Below: Panoramic view of a Vaenga dispersal, with Hurricanes of 151 Wing heavily muffled against the searing cold, and equally well protected RAF personnel taking the opportunity for a sled tow.

Squadron, with Turner as F/Sgt in charge. One complete Flight of 504(F) Sqdn under S/Ldr Rook formed the other squadron (No 81) to complete Wing under W/Cdr Isherwood. Wing to be equipped with Hurricane IIB aircraft. Main party of Wing left Leconfield to embark on August 13th, but the Carrier party (24 pilots) left for Glasgow on the 16th and joined HM Aircraft Carrier *Argus* on 18th. *Argus* left Glasgow on the morning of 19th and arrived at Scapa Flow the next day to pick up the escort.

Scapa Flow—Visited HMS *Prince of Wales* on Aug 22nd, and HMAC *Victorious* the next day. Remained at Scapa for a week or so before proceeding on our journey.

Journey from Scapa to Murmansk, USSR
Left Scapa on morning of Aug 30th and, escorted by cruiser *Shropshire* and three *Tribal* Class destroyers, set out for Ice- land. Reached Iceland on 31st, but fog so thick that convoy did not attempt to refuel there, but pushed off towards Spitzbergen to rendezvous with HMAC *Victorious* and two cruisers and three destroyers.

Sept 1st
Thick fog and convoy proceeding at reduced speed.

Sept 2nd
As previous day; fog still thick. At mid- day position somewhere about 73N 8W.

Sept 3rd
Time for rendezvous with *Victorious* fixed at 20.00hrs. Fog still thick during morning but cleared towards evening. Received news that two Fulmars from *Victorious* had destroyed a Dornier 17 and also that the *Victorious* and convoy were being shad- owed. Fog returned with evening and rendezvous not effected.

Hurricane IIb of 151 Wing housed in its 'shanty-type' wood hangar, Vaenga. Overhead a Russian SB3 bomber comes in to land.

Sept 4th

Weather clear up to about 10.00hrs, but patches of fog later in day. Joined with *Victorious*'s convoy early in the day. Several flaps when Fulmars or Martlets scrambled as convoy still being shadowed. Owing to shadowing, original course altered, and whole convoy (11 ships) headed NE towards Franz Josefland.

Sept 5th

Still proceeding NE and at 09.00 hrs reached position 78N 40.40 E, when we turned due E. At about 12.00hrs altered course to SE and headed towards Norgan Jembla (sic).

Sept 6th

Still heading S. towards Russian coast. Weather bad and sea very rough.

Sept 7th

Arrived at position 69.30N:33.10E and flew off *Argus* by Flights to proceed to Vayenga (sic) aerodrome. CO led first Flight but unfortunately F/Lt Berg and Sgt Campbell hit the ramp at end of flight deck, breaking two undercarriages. Both machines crash-landed on arrival. I led B Flight, 134, and arrived quite OK (0730, Hurricane Z3763).

RUSSIA

Sept 8th

No flying done as main party had not arrived from Archangel with necessary equipment. Started organising dispersal points and living accommodation. In evening were invited by the Russian General commanding local forces to a banquet to meet the 'brave Russian pilots' who had shot down '15 or more' of the 'enemy crafts' each. Evening quite successful, everyone toasting everyone else, but the whole Wing passed out completely after drinking vodka. I was so bad I completely missed the concert given in our honour.

Right: A Russian pilot tries his hand at running the engine of an 81 Squadron Hurricane at Vaenga.

Centre right: Hurricane talk. Squadron Leader A. G. Miller, OC 134 Squadron (in greatcoat, centre) chats with the noted Soviet fighter pilot, Captain Safanov (with 'chute) and other 'student' Russians. Behind Miller are two members of 134, who helped 'convert' the Russians on to Hurricanes, Pilot Officer Elkington (in fur jacket) and Flight Lieutenant J. K. Ross, DFC.

Right: 151 Wing personnel, mainly the non-flying officers. From left: Flt Lt Hubert Griffiths (Wing adjutant); Flt Lt V. A. Cottam (Senior interpreter); Flt Lt Murphy (Equipment); Flt Lt Willis (Cyphers); Flt Lt Gordon (Accounts); Sqn Ldr A. G. Miller (OC 134 Squadron); Plt Off Pratt (Cyphers); Wg Cdr H. N. G. Ramsbottom-Isherwood, DFC, AFC (151 Wing commander); Sqn Ldr A. H. Rook (OC 81 Squadron); Flt Lt Hodgson (Interpreter); Fg Off Goodman (Cyphers); Flt Lt Gittins (Engineering); Plt Off Nicholls (Cyphers); Flt Lt Fisher (Signals— kneeling). The pet 3½ months old reindeer was named 'Droochok' ('Little Friend'). Photo taken November 14th, 1941.

Sept 9th
Wing spent practically whole day in bed, thoroughly ill after previous night. Did not eat anything all day. No flying done.

Sept 10th
Still completing armament of aircraft and painting on letters. Dispersals getting fit to live in. Weather not very good.

Sept 11th
11.30. 134 Sqdn came to Readiness in morning. B Flight (Self, Cameron, Furneaux and Melann) led by a Russian Captain (Kuharenko) patrolled from Vayenga to the Finnish frontier and along the front. Considerable activity observed on front, mostly artillery fire. No enemy aircraft encountered. Russian pilot flying an I.20 aircraft. Self flying aircraft Y (Z3763) had engine cut three times over enemy territory due to inferior quality of Russian petrol (95 Octane) but managed to return OK.

Sept 12th
11.15. B Flight patrolled Zone 4 but saw nothing. 81 Sqdn fired at Me 110.

Sept 12th
14.00. Hurricane Z3763,Y. B Flight again patrolled Zone 4 and along front. No activity anywhere. Later in day 81 Sqdn again had luck and shot down two 109s

destroyed, two damaged.

Sept 14th
Z3763,Y. 14.00. One He 126 destroyed. B Flight dispersal becoming organised and more like home.

Sept 15th
Z3763,Y. 10.45. Squadron continuing front line patrols, but as yet no luck at all.

Sept 16th
No flying owing to weather. Vayenga definitely a dump.

Sept 17th
Z3763,Y. 11.55. Squadron beginning to escort Russian bombers on raids over the lines. This at least should reproduce results.

Sept 17th—23rd
Very little flying carried out owing to bad weather. Two heavy falls of snow on 22nd & 23rd. Visited Murmansk, but found it definitely a dump also.

Sept 24th
Z3763,Y. 11.55. Escorted four Russian bombers to bomb AA position, just west of the line. No E/A sighted. Only AA. B Flight only, self leading.

Sept 26th
Z3763,Y. 17.15. Captains Safanov and Kuharenko first solos. Self and Cameron patrolled round front line to try and sniff out a little trouble. No luck, not even AA.

59

Sept 27th

Z3763,Y. 07.20. B Flight patrolled front line during early morning looking for trouble. Found it by way of AA—very fierce and accurate. Flight patrolling at about 2,000ft scattered wildly but reformed soon after. Thought I was hit once as engine coughed and emitted black smoke. B Flight acted as high cover to A Flight, who escorted four Russian bombers to bomb front line. A Flight sighted 109, but we saw nothing. F/Lt Berg took off at approx. 15.00hrs on a scramble with two men on his tail. Aircraft spun in from 100 ft. Both men killed and Berg injured. In evening B Flight escorted five Russian bombers to bomb in Zone 1. No activity observed.

Sept 28th

Z3763,Y. 17.35. Escorted seven Russians to bomb in Zone 1. B Flight close escort, self leading. A Flight as top cover. Both Flights crossing over top of bombers. Bombing appeared quite good. Extensive AA but no EA activity.

Sept 29th

Z3763. 17.50. No activity from EA but very heavy AA during escort for three Russian bombers. One bomber shot down, crew baled out. Captains Safanov and Kuharenko local flying. Safanov made Hero of Soviet Union (Gold Star).

Oct 1st

No operational flying. Flew Russian Y-2 biplane for few minutes with Captain Kuharenko. Safanov and Kuharenko local flying and both getting to like Hurricane.

Oct 2nd

Z3763. 17.55. Went to investigate 'noise above cloud' but found nothing. Safanov and Kuharenko flew Hurricanes—aerobatics mostly. Safanov to instruct other Russian pilots.

Oct 3rd, 4th & 5th

Weather bad. No operational flying. Russians did not attempt to fly.

Oct 6th

Aerodrome attacked by 14 Ju 88s, escorted by 109s, while A Flight was practice flying. Cameron two damaged; Furneaux $\frac{1}{2}$ confirmed (with Rook); Barnes and Elkington one confirmed. F/Lt Rook one Me 109 confirmed. Several more damaged. B Flight aircraft took off during bombing. Aerodrome machine-gunned at same time. 134's score, $1\frac{1}{2}$ destroyed and three

probables. Safanov taught Captains Palcoonikov and Pogarielli to fly Hurricanes. Pogarielli pranged aircraft and broke wing tip.

Oct 7th

Weather bad. No ops. Pogarielli local flying. Russians broke second Hurricane.

Oct 8th

Z3763. 11.40. Bomber escort. B Flight close cover to seven Russian bombers, A Flight high cover. Bombed aerodrome over Finnish frontier. Only one EA seen. Having landed only 15 minutes, ordered B Flight patrol Zones 2–4. Several Ju 88s about but none sighted—cloudy.

Oct 9th

Snowed hard all day, no flying.

Oct 10th & 11th

Snowed hard both days. Russians flew Hurricanes in between snow-storms.

Oct 12th

Z3763. 16.00. Weather cleared towards evening. B Flight patrolled Zone 1 to intercept four Me 110s reported to be attacking front line. No 110s seen. No AA.

Hurricane IIb, Z3768 of 134 Squadron, being overflown by a Vic of 151 Wing's other Hurricanes. The ground conditions, even in relatively 'warmer' conditions, were a severe test of the aircraft's ruggedness.

Oct 13th

Weather fairly good all day, but cloud fairly low. Squadron detailed to escort SBs to bomb Target No. 13 but this op cancelled owing to weather conditions. Several new Russian pilots went solo on Hurricane. B Flight, 134 Squadron still acting as OTU for Russians.

Oct 14th

Fog all day, no flying of any kind.

Oct 15th

Z3763. 16.35. B Flight did voluntary stand-by at 1530hrs owing to report of four Ju 88s having crossed line. At 1610 were told the flap was over—and immediately afterwards 88s bombed Murmansk. Took off immediately but of course we were too late. Definitely a case of bad control. Snow-storms.

Oct 16th

Z3763. 13.15. Bomber escort for seven Russians to bomb target at western end of Zone 1. A Flight close cover, and B Flight crossing over 2,000ft above (14,000 ft). Weather perfect over German lines.

Only one burst of AA. This is thought to have been a signal to enemy fighters of our presence. Fighters however did not appear. At about 1530hrs smoke trails seen near lines and shortly afterwards Ju 88s came over aerodrome and dropped seven bombs on same. Control of course knew nothing until bombs fell, so once again squadron took off amid falling bombs, but we were too late to catch 88s.

Oct 17th

Z3763. 0930. Squadron (self leading) detailed to escort three SB3 and four SB2s to bomb east of Petsamo. Flights flew in cross-over cover and raid successfully carried out. No AA or enemy fighters.

This was last day of operations for B Flight as Russians took over our aircraft next day to form No 1 Russian Hurricane Squadron, under Senior Lieutenant Yakovenko. Wing of three Russian Hurricane squadrons formed by October 19th, led by Captain Safanov, with Captain Kuharenko second in command. We sailed from Vayenga on November 28th.

Armament

Full Blast. The effect of eight Browning .303 machine guns spectacularly illustrated by this night shot.

Right: Starboard wing gun installation of a Hurricane I, showing the four Browning .303 guns and their associated ammunition feed chutes.

Below: Ammunition was usually delivered from a Maintenance Unit already belted and in boxes, but armourers in front-line squadrons (when facilities existed) ran all belts through a Belt Positioning Machine (as here) to ensure positive alignment of each round with the rest of the belt, thus eliminating one possible cause of jamming in the guns.

Left: Armourers
(nearest) and other ground
tradesmen refurbishing
Hurricane I, V7795, in the
Western Desert, North
Africa, 1942. This was one of
two Hurricanes titled *Alma
Baker Malaya*, being
'presented' (ie paid for) by
C. Alma Baker OBE, a lady
resident in Malaya. The
Browning guns and their
ammunition chutes can be
plainly seen on the wing,
prior to installation.

Centre: Armourers of an
Auxiliary Air Force squadron
(believed to be 601) lapping
in the .303 ammunition belts.
The tubes evident in the
leading edge were blast
tubes, inside which lay the
gun barrels when installed.

Below: Desert doings.
Conveying ammunition to
Hurricane P3728 of 33
Squadron at Fuka satellite
airfield, late 1940.

Above: Once serviced, harmonised and armed, the guns are tested for smooth operation in the station stop butt—in this case a rather elaborate brick edifice in the Middle East. The red flag hoisted above the butt indicated live firing in progress—just in case passers-by were deaf!

Centre: Stepped-up starboard echelon of 87 Squadron's Hurricane IIcs.

Above far right: Hurri-Bomber. BE417, AE-K of 402 Squadron (Canadian) at Warmwell, early 1942, being loaded with its complement of 250lb GP bombs. Note exhaust anti-glare panel and brick-red doped fabric patches over machine gun ports.

Below far right: Peel off. Hurricane IIcs of No 1 Squadron RAF 'flake off' for a ground strafe, circa September 1942, just prior to the unit's re-equipment with the Hurricane's successor and stable-mate, Hawker Typhoons.

Right: Heavier punch. A four 20mm cannon Hurricane IIc, BD867, QO-Y of 3 Squadron RAF displaying the barrels of its main armament. Note the cordite streaking under the wing.

Loaded for game. Hurricane
IIb, with two 250lb GP
bombs and 12 × .303
machine guns, ready for a
low-level sweep over
France, spring 1942.

Below: Muscle-power.
Loading the port wing
carrier of a 402 Squadron
Hurricane IIb, 'Q', at
Warmwell on February 9th,
1942. From left: LACs
J. Holland and P. Laroche;
Cpl L. Lott; LAC H.
McGuiniss. The bomb is a
250lb GP (General
Purpose), tail-fused.

Above: A late-series Mk IV, KZ706, fitted with the large 'Long Tom' RP rails for tests over Pendine Sands towards the end of the war. During initial trials with RP on Hurricanes, blast protection plates were fitted under the wings, but in the event were found to be superfluous.

Left: Rocket Battery. Hurricane IV, BP173, bearing eight three-inch rocket projectiles (each with a 60lb High Explosive head). Built originally as a IIb, this machine was modified by Hawkers to Mark IV specifically for RP trials and went to the A & AEE, Boscombe Down for such trials on July 29th, 1942.

Bottom left: Crutching down. Once hooked on to the carrier, the bomb was steadied by crutching down two pairs of pads above the bomb. Transit rings in the bomb noses here indicate tail fusing. The small housing inboard of the wing gun ports housed the G42 cine camera, wired electrically to the cockpit for either co-ordinated operation when guns were fired or triggered independently (camera only).

69

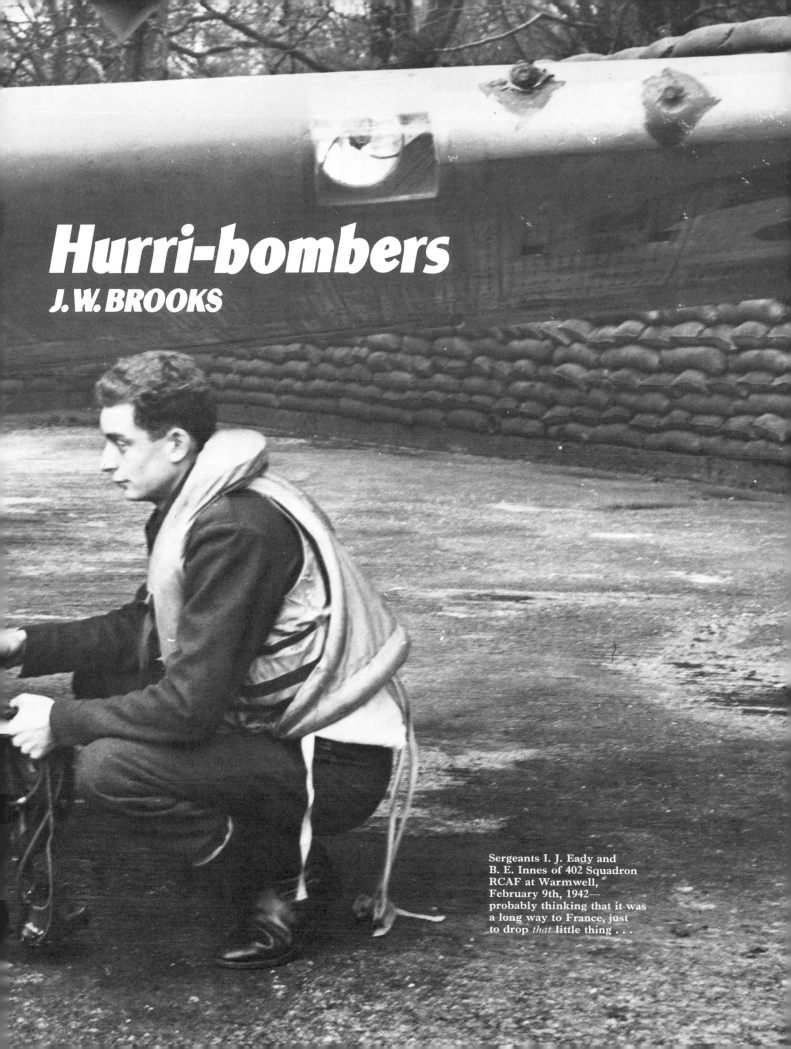

Hurri-bombers
J. W. BROOKS

Sergeants I. J. Eady and
B. E. Innes of 402 Squadron
RCAF at Warmwell,
February 9th, 1942—
probably thinking that it was
a long way to France, just
to drop *that* little thing . . .

How does one describe the feelings of flying a Hurricane? Remain objective and understandable, yet avoid nostalgia on the one hand and pure technicalities on the other? To even attempt it for someone who has never been a pilot would be virtually impossible—rather like trying to explain colour to a person who was born blind. The Hurricane was the first real war plane I flew and therefore holds a place in my memories which no other aircraft has taken, not even the Spitfire. It was the aircraft in which I learned the 'art' of staying alive because it was practically viceless, besides being very kind to ham-fisted beginners like myself. It could take enormous punishment, not only from its pilot but also from the opposition—something the delicate, feminine Spitfire would never do. One Hurricane I saw had the tail plane and elevators almost completely destroyed in a collision with a Messerschmitt 109, yet it flew over 100 miles across the Channel back to base at Manston. The stick movement was somewhat restricted, but it got down OK. The odd bullet hole through the fabric of the rear fuselage or control surfaces was not considered to be of any consequence and was patched up with a small square of fabric and red dope. After any long spell of ops, some of our Hurricanes looked as though they had caught some spotty disease, although this was very quickly 'cured' with dabs of green and brown paint after the red dope had dried.

Our Hurricanes (and Spitfires, of course) were always coloured with drab browns, greys and greens—for camouflage it was said. Yet our German counterparts always seemed bright and gay in contrast, with yellows and reds on silvery backgrounds. One *Geschwader* based at St Omer, known (I think) as 'Hermann Goering's Own', had the noses of their 109s painted a bright yellow as far back as the cockpit, together with splendid insignia in equally bright colours along each side. There seemed to be no attempt at concealment and one could see them quite plainly a distance away, with the sun glinting on their silver wings. They looked for all the world like model aircraft. However, the Hurricane's drab colours were of some use, and on two occasions saved me from what could have been nasty situations. I liked my drab colours.

To actually fly the Hurricane was a delight. A pilot had to find out for himself, since there was no dual-controlled Hurricane built (until much later). You simply got in and flew it and very few pilots ever came to grief during the first flight, It was later, when one found how 'easy' it appeared, that over-confidence replaced prudence and accidents occurred. No aircraft will put up with silly abuse by its pilot, not even the Hurricane, yet I believe it was the most forgiving. Because it had a tail wheel, as against the usual nose wheel of today's aircraft, a pilot could not see straight ahead when the Hurricane was on the ground and he had to look at an angle each side past the large nose. This meant one had to swing from side to side during taxying to spot any obstructions, such as chocks and other equipment which always seemed to clutter up airfields. On take-off, to keep straight, a pilot had again to look at an angle (I always looked to the left side) until the tail came into flying position, when one could see straight ahead. The Spitfire, especially the late Marks, were even worse than the Hurricane in this respect. Being a propeller aircraft, due to torque there was a pronounced swing which had to be held with rudder. This, coupled with the fact that one could not see straight ahead, could make things a little difficult—especially in a crosswind. Nevertheless, the controls were effective down to very low speeds and, after a few hours' handling, one hardly noticed these things. The tail came up quite quickly as one opened the throttle and within no time at all one was airborne. Compared with modern aircraft the take-off run was minute. We flew from grass fields not much bigger than a couple of football pitches and in our ignorance thought little about it.

Once in the air with the wheels up, the Hurricane was a delight. You didn't so much fly it as 'wear' it. The lightest touch on the controls was all that was needed and even this was done quite unconsciously. You appeared to think the aircraft into a turn or out of it. At high speeds the controls did tend to stiffen up and this was common on all aircraft. Yet the Hurricane could still be manoeuvred quite adequately. It was better than the Spitfire in this respect and far superior to the Messerchmitt 109. On the other hand it was slower than both of those aircraft, although more manoeuvrable. It could literally 'turn on a sixpence'. This was probably the reason that the Hurricane was considered ideal for tackling bomber formations, while the faster, sleeker Spitfire took on the escorting fighters. Unfortunately this 'arrangement' did not always work out in practice and Hurricanes had their work cut out with the later Marks of 109s and even more so with Focke-Wulf 190s. For this reason the Hurricane was relegated to defensive or fighter-bomber roles. It was sent on offensive sweeps in 1941 but was usually employed as close escort to Blenheim and Boston light bombers. These operations (known to the RAF as 'Circus') were primarily adopted to bring up the German fighters for the loosely-scattered Spitfire squadrons to scrap with. The Hurricanes' job was to fend for the bombers if the 109s got through—which they invariably did. I don't think these sweeps did any damage to the German war effort—the bomb load carried was far too small—but what they did do was to boost the morale of the RAF and the British people.

It was on one of these sweeps that a real ding-dong scrap took place. We Hurricanes had 109s passing through our formation, between individual aircraft, going in the opposite direction. Their tactics were to scream down from high above and make head-on attacks. Then, after passing through, to pull up, turn round and make another attack from the rear. The Hurricane escort couldn't leave the bombers, so we were easy prey for this sort of tactic. On one occasion I was attacked from the rear in this fashion. The 109 pilot badly misjudged his speed and/or mine and overshot. He then did a rather foolish thing—he pulled up to see where I'd gone and presented himself right in front of me, about 100 yards away. I simply fired and he blew up—I was most astonished.

Somehow the very ruggedness of the Hurricane's design seemed to give the pilot a sense of security, albeit a false sense. It was only made of sheet aluminium, wood and fabric, and one's only protection was the engine in front and a sheet of armour plate behind the seat. This latter, unfortunately, was not much good against the heavy cannons that German fighters carried. The 30mm Mauser firing through the prop boss in the case of the 109 made a nice neat hole as clean as a whistle. The Merlin engine which powered both the Hurricane and the Spitfire had one serious defect, when compared with the Daimler-Benz engine of the 109. The Merlin fuel system was carburetter-controlled (the SU carb), whilst the DB had fuel injection. This enabled a German pilot to bunt ie push his stick forward if he was being chased, whereas the Merlin would cut out completely under those circumstances. We had to roll over on to our backs and pull back on the stick, which was time-consuming and one lost sight of the target. Later Marks of Spitfire were fitted with fuel injection, but the Hurricane never was. The Hurricane could only be glided upside down, whereas a 109 could actually fly that way.

In late 1941 the Hurricane became a fighter-bomber and its prime job was purely low-level attacks on Channel shipping and against static targets over France and the Low Countries. It was fitted with a faired bomb rack under each wing, carrying (normally) two 250lb bombs. During the Dieppe raid this was doubled to two 500lb bombs—which was also the effective bomb load of the Blenheim and Boston light bombers! It was about then that skip-bombing was 'discovered'—the Americans 'rediscovered' it about a year or so later, much to our amusement. At Manston (my base) one squadron had bombs and 10 machine guns (.303) and the sister squadron had just four 20mm Oerliken cannons for armament. During a shipping strike the cannons went in first to shut up the opposition and the 'bombers' used to be right in behind them. Those convoys of smallish ships used to hug the coast and were always escorted by flak ships. These were modified tugs simply bristling with guns of all sorts and could put up an awful lot of hot metal. During any attack it was necessary to fly straight at the target, just skimming the waves and releasing the bombs at the last minute. Then one had to fly straight through all the heavy flak, hoping for the best. It was now that the Hurricane was most vulnerable. Underneath the pilot was a large radiator which if it got as much as a single bullet in it usually meant 'curtains'! The engine either seized up solid or caught fire. This meant that a pilot had to get out. Unfortunately one was too low to bale out and if you did have the speed to pull up, you were a sitting duck. The casualties in such raids were very high.

Favourite targets during late 1941 and early 1942 were the German air bases in France. The Hurricane was ideal for such work since it could fly very low (a couple of feet) and be jinked at the same time to avoid the ground defences. On a personal note, when flying the Hurricane under combat conditions I used to screw up the throttle friction nut tightly and then use both hands on the control column spade grip. This allowed one to use all one's strength in manoeuvres—although thinking back, the poor Hurricane must have been terribly strained at times.

One other type of operation which 607 Squadron used to do from Manston in early 1941 was night intruder. This called for single Hurricanes to go out at night to various German airfields in France and the Low Countries and wait around for returning German bombers. The Luftwaffe bases were often lit up like Christmas trees, having an approach and landing system called (I believe) Lorenz visual. This comprised a line of white lights leading to the runway in use, with cross-bars of other lights, usually coloured. The idea was that an approaching aircraft in bad visibility could line itself with the runway and descend as it crossed the coloured lights at a given height. There was also another squadron (No 1 ,RAF) at Manston with long-range Hurricanes painted black, whose sole task was night intrusion. Their most famous pilot was a Czech, Karel Kuttelwascher, who was reputed to have shot down many enemy aircraft over their own bases. The Hurricane was not easy to fly on instruments, particularly at night. It was preferable to have an horizon to go by and we always tried to operate when there was a moon on a nice clear night. We were all pretty 'green' at that time, with only a few hundred hours actual flying to our credit, but we all seemed to cope OK.

It was about that time (1941) that we started carrying the small rubber dinghies. It was put in a pack about four inches thick and was placed between the pilot and his parachute—dimensions being (as far as I remember) 18 inches by 12 inches by four inches. The inflation bottle was situated in the forward part of this pack, so that as a pilot moved his legs they rubbed against the inflating cock, a black, knurled ring. This, when turned or screwed down into the neck of the bottle, pierced a copper disc which in turn released gas and inflated the dinghy. Unfortunately, the constant leg movements on this bottle and cock had the effect of slowly wearing a hole in the copper disc, or at least wearing it thin. This could cause an unexpected discharge of the bottle and the dinghy to inflate in the cockpit. The pilot was thrust upwards and the central control column was pushed forward—the result of which was predictable. There were a lot of disasters before the reason was found, and then all pilots were issued with sharp, stabbing knives. It happened to me at night in the circuit over Manston. I was lucky, since I'd been on an op over France and was preparing to land when my dinghy inflated. I punctured it in record time with my knife but came very near to castrating myself. I was shaking a week later at the very thought . . .! Later, the inflation bottles were modified and put in a less vulnerable position.

The amount of personal equipment we used to carry on operations was really unbelievable. Apart from our uniform of blue battle dress, thick white socks, white roll-neck pullover (Navy type), fleece-lined flying boots, three pairs of gloves (one, white silk, then a woollen pair and overall leather gauntlets which were covered in something like varnish—fire-proofing), one leather helmet, oxygen mask-combined with microphone and heavy goggles; we had a yellow 'Mae West', a pack of escape money, iron ration pack containing glucose, barley sugar, an outfit for purifying water, small compass, a 'dirty' silk handkerchief(actually a map of France). Personal armament consisted of a revolver stuck down one boot and a Commando knife down the other. Under our battle dress we often had a civilian zipper jacket with a beret tucked away inside—though this was highly unofficial! We also had modified brass buttons on our trousers which could be used as makeshift compasses. Over all this lot one strapped on one's parachute/dinghy pack and somehow clambered into the Hurricane's cockpit. I've heard that the armoured knights of medieval times were hoisted on to their mounts by a sort of crane—I feel we could have usefully used something similar . . .!

Lastly, there was the task of landing a Hurricane. I'd like here to recall that a Hurricane was a 'first time' aeroplane, in the sense that you could not have dual instruction in it. Therefore, when you first landed, it was right after the time you took off and flew it for the first time. Instruction was all given on the ground before one got airborne. Once in the air you tried hard to remember all that you'd been told—though you usually forgot. Fortunately the undercarriage of the Hurricane was wide and very strong, unlike either the Spitfire and Me 109. It could be 'dropped' in without any undue harm. Nevertheless, it could at the same time be made to 'sit down' so gently that it became a matter of personal pride not to feel the aircraft touch the ground. And believe me, we used to operate from some rough old airfields—mostly grass, without concrete runways. I remember once during the summer of 1941 returning from a sweep escorting Blenheims and landing at Manston. A friend of mine, Sergeant Batchelor, had been badly shot up, particularly about the face and head. He flew his Hurricane back and landed it at Manston with the help of some squadron friends (who flew alongside him and talked him down) when he was almost blind. Later I heard that he became permanently blind. I saw all this whilst on the ground, resting beside my own aircraft. We were given lemonade by a party of Boy Scouts accompanied by a local vicar. (I wonder if any of those people still remember this . . . ?)

As with the take-off, one actually landed a Hurricane in the final stages by looking at an angle from straight ahead. The technique was to close the throttle and glide at around 100mph (we used instruments graded in mph, not knots as they are today calibrated). One never came in straight in line with the landing path (or runway) but in a continuous slight left-hand turn, side-slipping if necessary. Then straighten up at the last moment, a split second before actual touchdown, looking to the left to judge height above the ground. It sounds slightly difficult but in fact, after a bit of practice, it became quite automatic. We normally took off and landed in formations of three and four aircraft at once and thought nothing of it.

They Also Served

FRANK HARTLEY

Mudlarks. A pre-1939 scene as a Hurricane of 17 Squadron is man-handled out of the soggy surface of a grass dispersal area, during field exercises.

The contribution of the toiling ground crews of the Hurricane squadrons—as with all other RAF fighting units—cannot be measured in terms of awards and victories. Yet without their loyalty, courage and devotion to the job, such epics as the Battle of Britain might never have been won. The erks—a universal RAF nickname for the maintenance men and women—gave an invaluable service, one which can never be over-estimated. Nor were their working conditions merely a comfortable sinecure, leaving the air crews to face all the dangers. Whether on a windswept winter dispersal in France, the barren rock-dust airstrips of North Africa, or the steaming sweatbath of a Burmese jungle strip, the erks were as much 'in the front line' as many of their airborne comrades. Possibly epitomising such conditions was Manston aerodrome in the summer of 1940. Well within range of marauding Luftwaffe fighters and bombers, Manston thoroughly earned its soubriquet, 'Hell-fire Corner'. Bombed, strafed and almost obliterated by continuous raiding, the airfield continued to provide a forward defence position for RAF Fighter command, despite almost complete lack of normal facilities. It was to Manston that Frank Hartley was posted just as the Battle of Britain had petered out.

Far left: Installing the oxygen bottles. The airman on the wing is carrying round his shoulders a Service gas mask —usually stuffed with a tea flask, NAAFI 'wads' (cakes or rolls), towel and soap—if the eagle eye of any officious NCO could be avoided!

Left: The men behind the men behind the guns. The anonymous but vital ground crews of the RAF— exemplified here by the erks of one of 242 Squadron's Flights at Martlesham Heath in the spring of 1941.

Bottom left: Radio check. AC1 J. A. Peterson checks the R/T of a 401 Squadron RCAF Hurricane IIb at Digby on July 24th, 1941.

Below: Pilot out. An American pilot of 71 (Eagle) Squadron climbs out as the ground crew takes over charge of the aircraft.

Bottom: 'Two Six'—the standard cry in RAF language for extra hands for any heavy job. The equivalent in Polish could have applied in this scene as airmen of 306 Polish Squadron (the 'Wild Ducks') shove Hurricane II, V7118, UZ-V back to its dispersal pan for servicing.

In January 1941 I was posted to RAF Manston, Kent, along with four of my colleagues. Situated within sight of the French coast, Manston had been under enemy attack many times and had earned the nickname, 'Hell-fire Corner'. When we arrived it was dark, but here and there we could see evidence of past enemy action, the empty shell of the Airmen's Mess, several flattened huts, the remains of a bombed wash-house, and the camp swimming bath which had once been a covered building—now resembling an open-air lido, except for the fact that most of the glazed tiles were missing and the bath was empty, probably no longer watertight. Next morning we set out to report to our new unit. We looked out expecting to see Hurricanes or Spits dispersed around the airfield, but our hopes were dashed—the only aircraft in sight were three Air Sea Rescue Lysanders. Walking round the aerodrome, and just before reaching our new section, we really thought we had 'struck gold' at long last. Passing a closed hangar, we decided to investigate and, peeping through a gap between the doors, one of my colleagues called excitedly, 'Look boys. Hurriboxes!' We squeezed through the gap into the hangar—only to find that the 'Hurries' were merely good decoys.

Full Revs. Engine fitters give the Merlin of Hurricane IIb, Z3658, YO-N of 401 (*Ram*) Squadron RCAF full power. Digby, July 24th, 1941.

Centre: Air Vent trouble. Warrant Officer G. Carpenter (inevitably, 'Chippy') and Corporal K. Warren discuss the problem during a Major Inspection of a Hurricane IIb of 402 Squadron at Warmwell, February 9th, 1942.

Top right: Wheel change. LAC P. J. Turgeon attends to a faulty brake on the port wheel of a 401 Squadron IIb at Digby, July 24th, 1941, supervised by Sergeant Bob Fair.

Right: Corporal Trimble, 401 Squadron, Digby, doing a DI (Daily Inspection) on the instrument panel.

Our new unit proved to be a Servicing Flight—a group of ground personnel whose function was to attend to all visiting aircraft ie aeroplanes of all types which did not belong to Manston. Sometimes a fighter, sometimes a bomber, damaged in action or perhaps short of fuel, would lob in for attention prior to returning to base. Although by 1941, Manston was in a sorry state, it must nevertheless have been a welcome sight to many aircrews managing to 'just make it' back to British soil once again. We did not have to wait long before we saw some action, for it was only about our third day on the station when two Messerschmitt 109s flew low over the airfield. It was the first time I had seen a German low enough to see the black crosses and swastikas. It was also the first and only time I actually saw bombs leaving an aircraft. Fortunately the damage was of little consequence, just four small craters from light calibre bombs.

A few weeks after our arrival we were pleased to see a squadron of Hurricanes arrive. It was great to see them sweep low over the airfield, climb again and peel off before coming in to land. For a while this was Manston's resident fighter squadron and frequently they would go out over the Channel to protect Allied convoys, or

perhaps to attack enemy shipping. Many battles could be heard taking place out there, though these were usually too far away to see clearly. On one such occasion we were astounded to see a Junkers 87 circling the aerodrome with a mixture of Hurricanes and Spitfires, about six in all, spread around its tail. It looked as if the pilot, realising the hopelessness of the situation, had resolved to call it a day and land. He was actually making his approach when suddenly (or so it seemed) the Junkers' gunner decided to have a go, and as he opened up so did the fighters— and the Junkers crashed in a nearby field, killing its crew.

In the course of time our unit became known as No 2 R & R (Refuelling and Rearming) Party. Instead of dealing with just odd bods, we were handling several squadrons each day, as well as a goodly number of night bombers. On many occasions five or six squadrons of Spitfires and Hurricanes would land at Manston

direct from their own bases. Our R & R Party would top up the fuel, oil and oxygen and thereby enable the planes to leave England brim-full of fuel etc to strike deep into enemy-occupied France, sometimes returning to Manston to refuel and rearm in readiness for a further sweep the same day, or perhaps just to return to their respective bases. In order to increase our fighters' range of penetration into German-occupied territory, the auxiliary (jettison) fuel tank was introduced. In the case of the Hurricane these cigar-shaped tanks were fitted under the wings near the fuselage. The idea was for the pilot to use the fuel in his jettison tanks first, then switch to his main tanks when the auxiliary supply was exhausted. If he met enemy fighters the pilot could, if necessary, jettison the auxiliary tanks and join in the fray or take evasive action unhampered. Speaking from memory, I think most of our machines returned to base complete with their jettison tanks—empty, but still attached.

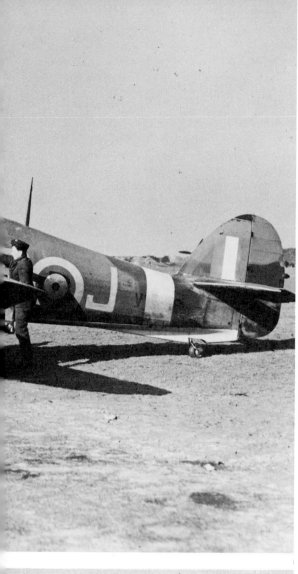

Perhaps one of the greatest attributes of the Hurricane lay in its capacity to absorb punishment and still fly. The fuselage aft of the cockpit was fabric-covered and it was not unusual to find bullet or shrapnel holes in this area, which could easily be repaired providing that the interior airframe structure and equipment were undamaged. Similar damage to a stressed skin (ie metal-covered) aircraft, such as the Spitfire, needed more time to effect a suitable repair. I have a vivid recollection of one Hurricane landing with tail planes, elevators and rudder reduced to a mere framework, with pieces of fabric hanging loose. As we surveyed the damage I remember thinking that this kite had defied all the known laws of aerodynamics, as its pilot had coaxed it home. A day or so later the Duke of Kent visited Manston, inspected this aircraft and chatted with the pilot. Sadly it must be recorded that this same pilot was killed within the next few days when practice bombing an exposed wreck in the Channel, off Pegwell Bay; while the Duke of Kent lost his life in an air crash in Scotland a few weeks later.

As the war progressed so the frequency of our fighter sweeps over enemy-held territory increased, shooting up supply lines, bombing bridges, roads, railway lines, attacks on enemy depots and the like. One morning, having refuelled a Hurricane in readiness for a daylight sweep, I chatted to the pilot concerning the destructive power of his four Hispano 20mm cannons. He described a raid on a German depot. His squadron was to attack in threes, each group in turn peppering the building with cannon fire, and then circle and repeat this attack. 'As I made my second approach,' he said, 'the face of the building collapsed like a jig-saw puzzle and I could see some of the floors sagging.' Attacks by Hurricanes were by no means confined to the day time. There was in fact a period when a Hurricane night fighter squadron operated from Manston with great success, particularly in moonlight periods. Thinking back, I can recall the names of two pilots of this unit, Flight Lieutenant Stevens and Sergeant Scott.

A rather awe-inspiring incident occurred one morning when a Hurribomber was making an approach to land, complete with

Far left: Run-up. Hurricane XII, 5658, 'B' of the RCAF at Dartmouth, Nova Scotia on May 6th, 1943. The mini-spinner on the propeller was common to most Canadian Hurricanes of the period. Note unusual form of wheel chocks in use.

Left: Start up. The pilot of V7608, XR-J, of 71 Squadron about to run up his engine, Kirton-in-Lindsey, Lincolnshire in spring 1941. First of the three American 'Eagle' squadrons formed within the RAF, composed of 'neutral' Americans, 71 was formed at Church Fenton on September 9th, 1940 but only commenced operations as a unit in February 1941.

Below: 'Here they come'— the ground crews prepare to receive their pilots for a scramble take-off. Canadians of 402 Squadron race to their Hurricanes at Warmwell, whilst the airmen stand by with parachute harnesses at the ready, cockpit straps in position and trolley accumulators plugged in. Experience provided a silk-like co-ordination in teamwork, thus avoiding unnecessary time-wasting in getting the aircraft airborne.

two 250lb bombs under its wings. From the ground we could see that the under-carriage was not properly locked down, the starboard wheel swinging loosely in the breeze. We shouted and waved frantically, hoping to attract the pilot's attention—but to no avail. The Hurricane touched down on its port wheel, the starboard wing hit the ground, the propeller splintered and the whole aircraft spun round as the port wheel collapsed, nearly tipping the plane on its nose. We raced to help the pilot out of the cockpit. Fortunately he was unhurt but very shaken as he surveyed the wreckage—and was no doubt relieved mightily to see the two bombs, which had become detached, lying peacefully a few yards away! Another occurrence which remains vivid in my mind concerning Hurricanes at Manston was the occasion when a number of Messerchmitt 109s were reported somewhere in the vicinity and two Hurricanes took off *with* the wind! Very soon they were over the Channel and, after about 20 minutes, they returned. It was later reported that the Hurricanes had crept up behind the Germans, literally joined their formation, and at an opportune moment picked off three tail-enders before the enemy realised what was happening.

During 1941 Wing Commander T. P. Gleave took over as station commander of Manston. He was a very upright officer

There they go. 242 Squadron Hurricanes at Martlesham Heath in early 1941. In foreground is Z2588, a Mk II.

with a somewhat athletic carriage, but it was evident that he had suffered severe burn injuries. Naturally we were all curious to know something of his background. The Wingco was a very energetic man, always dashing from place to place, and it soon became obvious that he was happiest among the Hurricanes, whether they were stationed at Manston or just dropping in from ops. One day a lone Hurricane landed and as it parked the Wingco drove up to meet it. I believe he was out of his car before it had stopped rocking! The Hurricane was a 12-gun job and in a short time the Wingco was excitedly walking round it, trying out the controls—just like someone inspecting their first new car, though I should add

that this was by no means a new Hurricane. It transpired that this aircraft had been allotted for the Wing Commander's personal use and he was a very delighted man indeed. As a Wing Commander he was entitled to have his own initials on the sides of his aircraft in place of normal squadron identification codes, and it was my privilege to paint 'T.P.G.' on each side of the fuselage, plus a number of small swastikas below the cockpit—these indicating the number of enemy planes destroyed by the Wing Commander in combat. As the airframe fitter on this machine, I was frequently in personal contact with the CO, and many times he took off alone in the hope of bagging another German.

Start up. Flying Officer Sprague of 401 Squadron RCAF 'gives her the gun', Digby, July 1941. His personal insignia, just below the exhaust stubs, comprised a small cartoon serpent sitting in a champagne glass, centred on a coloured diamond shape.

174 Squadron's Hurri-
bombers at Manston in May
1942. Known as the
'Mauritius Squadron', XP-Y
is BE684 and XP-G is BE421.
Dieppe cost this unit dear,
nearly half of the participat-
ing pilots being lost.

Operation Jubilee
J. W. BROOKS

I was based at Manston in Kent with 174 Squadron and flew the 'new' Hurribombers. 'New' in the sense that the Hurricane was by then considered as outclassed by the new German fighters, so it was fitted with bombs—one 250lb under each wing. The squadron by then was fully operational and experienced in low-level work, and although the chop rate was high, there was no lack of enthusiasm. So when we were sent to Ford on a temporary posting, along with a number of other Hurricane and Spitfire squadrons, we knew something big was on. I see from my log book that I made an entry, 'To Ford, for what?' That was on August 14th.

We had no idea of what we were supposed to do, except that it was fighter-bomber work. However, it wasn't very difficult to reason out our target. Since we knew we were to operate from Ford, and knew our effective range, our most obvious destination was in the Dieppe-Fecamp area.

On the evening of August 18th we were all carefully briefed about what was to happen next day. We were told, amongst other things, that the German reaction was liable to be quick and massive. I personally can't remember very much of that briefing after all this time, except that this was not going to be *the* invasion but merely a 'try-out'. We were told that our job was

to cover the landings of Canadian troops etc. What did dismay our particular squadron was that we were to be the first lot in, before first light. We were also told that we were going to dive-bomb our targets at low level, and that we were to have two 500lb bombs instead of our usual two 250lb—just twice the weight. I was a Section leader at this time and was detailed with my three other pilots to dive-bomb some heavy naval-type guns which were emplaced to the rear of Dieppe on some high ground. These, we were told, could cover the beaches and sea approaches and it was essential to knock them out at first go. Which accounted for our early departure.

On the morning of the 19th we were called at some ghastly hour, although few of us had slept much that night. After a scratch breakfast served by the ever-ready WAAFs, we got into our aircraft already warming up on the airfield. Since we were taking off in the dark we had to have our navigation lights on to see each other, this being a real novelty to us. It was also remarkable that we had no collisions since we always took off in formation, four at a time. I believe there were three Sections to our squadron effort (12 aircraft) although there may have been another four aircraft on a separate job. My own Section formed up behind me in close formation

so that they couldn't lose me in the dark, and I kept a close eye on our new CO, Squadron Leader Fayolle, a Free French pilot, whose father was (I believe) an admiral in pre-war France. He had been with us just a few weeks. We flew in low since there was still a need not to alert the Germans of our approach—the first of our troops had not yet landed.

It took us about 40 minutes to cross to the other side but long before we got there I could see a fire. This turned out to be a German ship which accidentally ran into the invasion fleet and had to be destroyed. Squadron Leader Fayolle naturally saw there was no need for us to continue on the deck, since the Germans obviously knew something was up, so we all climbed up to a couple of thousand feet in order to pin-point ourselves and to get sufficient height to dive with our bombs. It was quite easy to make out the coast and the town of Dieppe. The ship on fire lit up the whole scene clearly and the flak and fireworks were on a par with November 5th. My Section broke off from the CO's, who had other targets, and I swung away to the northern side of Dieppe. I dropped down to 1,500 feet and told the Section to drop back in line-astern, ready for diving. All this had been planned beforehand, needless to say, so that there was a minimum of R/T natter and less chance of confusion.

The light flak was coming up thick and fast and we were flying at a very vulnerable height. I could see the 40mm stuff curving up towards us, for all the world like a strike of bright glowing beads on a string. It would flash past us and explode just above our heads—or so it appeared. Flak always looked worse at night. We were the only aircraft in the area so we knew it was meant for us alone. I was trying hard to remember the target details from our briefing, what it looked like and more important where it was. Then I saw it. Three or four big splodges of concrete surrounded by trees. I called up my Section and told them 'target ahead' although I found out later that they had seen it at the same time as myself, so they were ready for my 'Tallyho'.

Some light flak came up from the gun site but it wasn't really enough to put us off. My main concern was that we would all pull out and miss the surrounding trees—this being the first time we had done formation dive-bombing at night, and with 1,000lb of bombs apiece. I went down as low as I dared to release my bombs—I couldn't really miss. I could make out the heavy guns on their white concrete bases, along with some smaller gun sites and huts. It was these smaller sites from which the guns were firing at me, so I fired back as I dived down. This was a general tactic to make the people on the ground keep their heads down. Eight machine guns all going at once are quite noisy. I pulled out at a couple of hundred feet and saw the trees loom out of the darkness in front of me. I was weaving like mad now just above the tree tops with lots of machine gun and 40mm stuff quite thick all around me. My bombs had 6-seconds delay fuzes, whilst the boys behind me had 2-second fuzes. This was to prevent those behind me being blown up by my bombs. Nevertheless it meant a quick and co-ordinated run over the target even with such precautions.

After what seemed a very long time, I saw the whole site go up in a series of quick flashes and then felt the crump, which bounced my Hurricane about. On my left I saw one of my Section having a hard time with the flak. He was weaving like a madman just over the tree tops—then he must have seen me and pulled over, to our mutual comfort. It was 'Tommy' Thomas. We were later joined by another of our Section and the three of us swung round to the south side of Dieppe. We all continued to machine-gun anything that moved on the ground. By then it was light enough to see and we all had a go at some German transport which disgorged its troops in a great big hurry. I could see a lot of activity on the sea and beaches. The German ship was still burning away merrily, although there were a lot of fires in the town and on the sea front. The troops were now landing and I could see the landing barges and other sea transports quite clearly. I flew out to sea, giving the Navy a wide berth since those chaps were (understandably) trigger-happy and let fly at anything in the air. I joined up with some more from 174 Squadron and we all continued back to Ford. Half-way back it was fully light and I counted seven Hurricanes from our squadron. I knew who they were by their aircraft code letters—mine was usually 'G'.

There was a lot of activity when I got back to Ford. The Spitfire squadrons were taking off and forming up into Wing formations before setting out. I was somewhat short of fuel and lost no time in getting in. Some other members of 174 arrived back in twos and threes, but three didn't come in—the new CO, Squadron Leader Fayolle, and Flight Sergeant James who was in my Section, plus one from the other Section. I should point out that on operations of the sort that 174 was engaged in, the turnover of pilots was so great that sometimes you hardly got to know a new chap before he was killed or went missing. It was said that if you managed to survive your first three ops then you had a good chance of completing your tour. All of our aircraft were found to have holes in them. My own 'G' had a few through the fabric which the ground staff were hastily patching over with red dope. Our greatest worry was getting hit in the radiator. If a single bullet punctured this, things happened very quickly. Within minutes your engine either seized solid, caught fire or simply blew up. In any event you had to get out in a hurry. Unfortunately the low-level nature of our work did not give us much chance since we couldn't bale out, while if we pulled up we were sitting targets for the ground flak.

Another two Sections from our squadron went out, led by the senior Flight commander, Flight Lieutenant MacConnell, now acting CO. These pilots had not been in the earlier detail and we told them what to expect. We heard from the returning Spitfires that there was a lot of scrapping with the Germans, particularly with the St Omer and Abbeville boys. After being debriefed by our Intelligence officer, Flying Officer Tunks, we all went off for a second breakfast and a rest in the sunshine. Sometime after lunch we were briefed to go out again. This time our target was a concentration of tanks and guns which were apparently moving in from north of Dieppe. We were also informed that our troops were now pulling out and we were supposed to cover them as best we could. Flight Lieutenant MacConnell was

Sergeants I. J. Eady and B. E. Innes of 402 Squadron RCAF at Warmwell, February 9th, 1942— probably thinking that it was a long way to France, just to drop *that* little thing . . .

to lead our eight serviceable Hurricanes.

A different sight now met my eyes when we arrived over Dieppe. At 1,500 feet I had a panoramic view in the brilliant sunshine. There was an extraordinary amount of rubbish floating around in the water, quite some way off-shore. There were bright yellow dinghies which stood out against a surface of oil and sundry junk. The German boat was still there and still smoking. It was quite small, or so it appeared. There was a dogfight going on overhead and we all kept our eyes peeled for an attack. It was our job to avoid any conflict as this meant we would have to get rid of our two bombs and hence our mission would be wasted.

We went in two lines abreast as pre-arranged and I could see the targets right ahead. They were slinging everything at us, or so it appeared. In the daytime it was difficult to see the amount of flak being fired at you, so if you were sensible you kept jinking about, not flying straight and level for one moment, and getting down as low as possible. I saw one of our Hurricanes get hit and catch fire. He dived straight at a bunch of armoured vehicles and blew up. I think this was a friend of mine called 'Doofy' du Fretay, a Free Frenchman who loathed Germans. Then another friend, an Australian named Flight Sergeant Watson who had been to my home in London, blew up. I think one of his bombs got hit as he went in. I flew straight at some transport and troops with my guns going and skipped my bombs at them. I passed over the top at a couple of feet and brought back with me a souvenir—the whip aerial of a German tank, wedged in my radiator. I wasn't sorry to get out of that lot and, together with Murray ('Tommy') Thomas, joined up with Flight Lieutenant MacConnell and we then went on a strafing run up to the coast.

We formed up to go home (there were now just five of us) at about 200 feet, when I saw to my horror a big formation of Messerschmitt 109s and Focke-Wulf 190s flying parallel to the coast. They passed directly over the top of us at not more than about 200 feet. It was possible to make out the individual markings, and one I noticed had a big black oil streak underneath. I held my breath, as I'm sure the

others did, since we had used most of our ammunition in the ground attacks. Besides this we would have been slaughtered, being outclassed, outnumbered and short of fuel. I watched them disappear into the smoke and confusion to the north. Then there was a Junkers 88 attacking a destroyer but all his bombs missed and threw up great columns of water. He was too fast for us and got away. It was nice to see the

BN114, loaded with 500lb GP bombs. Though seen here at Boscombe Down in March 1942, this aircraft served later with 451 Squadron, RAAF in Cyprus and Egypt.

Bottom left: Replenishment. 250lb GP bombs are fitted to a Hurricane IIb for another sortie across the Channel. The wooden hand transporter was a 'local' aid constructed by the unit's armourers.

English coast again and even nicer to get down in one piece, because I was sure I'd been hit somewhere vital. In fact all I had was a lot more holes in 'G' and she was still flyable. We had been on the ground only a short time when a Ju 88, or a Dornier, came over Ford at very low altitude and dropped a stick of bombs straight across the grass. He ducked in and out of some low cloud which was coming in from the sea. He was a very brave man. I think he was later shot down by a Beaufighter. Around tea time we were stood down as the operation was considered over as far as we were concerned. We had lost Squadron Leader Fayolle, Pilot Officers du Fretay and van Wymeersch, Flight Sergeants Watson and James, and two others whose names escape me. We had begun the operation with (I think) 17 pilots, and we now had eight left and some very patched Hurricanes. Next day we flew back to Manston.

Malta Defender
FRED ETCHELLS

'Collie's Battleship'—L1669, a Hurricane I which was the only Hurricane in the Western Desert in June 1940, attached to 80 Squadron. So-named because it represented Air Commodore (then) Ray Collishaw's only modern fighter. Seen here in England, prior to leaving for Egypt.

Fred Etchells probably holds some form of record for longevity of Hurricane operational experience. He flew them from December 1940 until March 1945, interspersed with many other fighter types. And those four years included operations in virtually every main variety of Hurricane on sweeps over the Channel, Malta defence and intruder sorties over Sicily instructing in Egypt, defence duties in Iraq, the Persian Gulf and Palestine operations from Syria and Cyprus and, finally, back to the UK. Perhaps understandably, his affection for the Hurricane remains vivid even today—yet one more example of the feeling engendered by the Hurricane in its myriad pilots. After several months of operations with 242 Squadron, Etchells was posted to 249

Right: Peel-off. An interesting study in underside markings (black and white) as a 213 Squadron Hurricane aerobats over the ill-fated island of Crete, 1941.

Above/right: Two views of 274 Squadron circa June–July 1940. Second pilot from right in first scene is Flying Officer P. G. Wykeham-Barnes (who eventually retired from the RAF as Air Marshal Sir Peter Wykeham), who played a leading part in the first two years of the desert air war, and ended the war as a Group Captain with 2nd TAF.

Squadron on May 7th, 1941, bound (ostensibly) for the Far East, and four days later flew in to Luqa airstrip on Malta Here, the squadron was 'retained'—the beginning, in Etchell's case, of some three long years of continuing service around the Mediterranean theatre of operations.

'Hullo my darling—third door on the right' was the greeting I'll never forget from a very elderly-looking sailor on duty at the top of a gangplank leading from a Liverpool dockside to an opening in the side of the aircraft carrier, *HMS Furious*. RAF tales of naval personnel, which until then I'd considered fabrications, came rushing into my mind! Very heavily laden with kitbag, suitcase and sundry other items, I approached the open door with caution—and in about 10 seconds flat had received a yellow fever inoculation to add to my long list of jabs required to prepare me for overseas service. I had recently left Douglas Bader's squadron, 242, flying Hurricane IIs, and joined 249 Squadron, equipped with tropicalised Hurri Is fitted with long range tanks. This was considered a great come-down after flying Mk IIs, which were a considerable improvement on the old Hurri Is. We believed we were heading for Singapore, and our 24 Hurricanes had been dismantled, taken aboard *Furious*, reassembled and crammed into a hangar below the flight deck. I had not

heard of Hurricanes taking off from aircraft carriers, and was very intrigued. I'm sure that a blind faith in the Hurricane must have dismissed any fears.

Greenock was our first port of call, where we took on fresh water and were away again within an hour or so. Then Gibraltar, where we moored at the dockside on to *HMS Ark Royal* (which by then had been 'sunk' about three times by Dr Goebbels), and shortly after arrival we pilots helped push our Hurricanes over a bridge of planks joining the two ships. As soon as this chore was completed the *Ark Royal* cast off and headed west into the Atlantic (to fool observers in local trawlers etc who reported all shipping movements to the Germans—or so we were told). In the middle of the night a sharp turn through 180 degrees and through the straits of Gibraltar—briefing next day for the first leg of our flight (which was to be to Malta for refuelling and rest)—packing kit into ammunition recesses and any odd spots

in the fuselage we could find—then all set for the 'Off' at dawn.

All 24 of our Hurricanes were tightly, crowded at the 'blunt end' of the carrier and I remember even now my almost complete disbelief at the impossibly short 'runway'. *Ark Royal* then opened her throttles and headed into wind at something like 30 knots, which meant a further 30-mph by the aircraft would give us the 60-mph needed for take-off. Conscious of the heavily-laden state of my machine, I was grateful for the great height of the flight deck above sea level, which had made me quite dizzy when looking over the side earlier in the journey. It meant no immediate necessity to climb until adequate flying speed was gained. I still recall the joy of seeing the aircraft in front of me become safely airborne before reaching the end of the flight deck at the 'sharp end'. Many of our pilots swore they bent their throttle levers to ensure maximum possible revs!

First squadron in the Middle East to receive a complement of Hurricanes was 274, which reformed at Amriyah on August 19th, 1940 with a mixture of Gloster Gladiators and Hurricanes, under the command of Sqn Ldr P. H. Dunn, DFC. The squadron recorded its first combat victory on September 10th, 1940. This scene was at Amriyah in late 1940, the nearest aircraft being P2544, YK-T.

Below: P2627, another of 274 Squadron's early equipment, over the barren desert hinterland, November 1940.

Our Hurricanes were being led by a Fleet Air Arm Fulmar, which was forced to return to the carrier after 45 minutes with engine trouble. But before long a replacement Fulmar met us and we turned round and again headed for Malta. After almost five and a half hours in the air, during which time two enemy aircraft crossed our track heading for Tunisia from Sicily, we saw Malta ahead—in the middle of a bombing raid by Italians from Sicily. We had been briefed to circle a small island off the south coast called Filfla, in order to identify ourselves, but the state of our fuel gauges decided the issue and we flew straight in to land at the first aerodrome sighted—Luqa in my case and several others, though others landed at Hal Far and Ta Kali. The anti-aircraft defences were firing at maximum rate and we were lucky to escape any hits on the squadron. 'Heads down' was the first desire after landing and taxying as close as possible to the nearest slit trench, where we hurriedly joined the RAF ground crews to whom air raids had become part of everyday life. After the raid we were gathered together and informed that instead of refuelling and continuing our journey to the Far East, we were needed more in Malta, and our base would be Ta Kali. The official promise was that we would do 12 months on the island and then return to the UK. For several of us it was to be three and a half years before we saw home again . .

Malta's air defence was in poor shape, and most of 249's pilots felt they were just the boys to remedy this defect, and morale was high. Our Hurricane Is were in good shape and we dreamed of meeting flocks of Stukas and slow, outdated Italian bombers, unescorted. The Axis, however, appeared to decide that as Malta had been reinforced, they would stiffen their aggression by adding Luftwaffe units to the Italian air forces, and we soon found Messerschmitt 109s to be more aggressive than the Macchi 200s as bomber escorts. The Junkers 88 was a superb aircraft for its purpose, and we found that if we intercepted a high raid after they had bombed, we could not catch them after they had their noses down by about 10 degrees, and they were soon back over the 60 miles of sea separating Malta from Sicily. After considerable losses on both sides, activity by the enemy was greatly reduced, which was fortunate for 249 Squadron in particular in view of the small number of Hurricanes available for duty. Towards the end of June 1941 we received reinforcements in the shape of Hurricane IIs, with fresh pilots to replace our casualties. The Mk IIs still could not cope with a nose-down Ju 88, but we had a much-improved performance at higher altitudes, which gave us a far greater chance of attacking raids from above.

Late summer saw some of our Hurri IIs fitted with Light Series bomb racks, holding four 40lb bombs under each wing, and a number of raids were carried out during moonlight nights on airfields in Sicily. The bomb racks appeared to upset the magnetic compasses and arrival at any intended aerodrome target was mainly a matter of luck. Nevertheless, enemy airfields were bombed and strafed. The Hurri

II had heavy fire-power in the shape of four 20mm cannons and obtained good results in many cases—setting fire to aircraft on the ground, petrol bowsers and buildings. One such raid gave rise to an eventual joyful reunion at a much later date. A fellow Flight Sergeant pilot was thought to have been shot down whilst strafing an airfield, and as no news came through to report his being taken prisoner, we mourned the loss of another comrade. Ten years later I was a guest at a golf club dinner, when the sight of my 'late' comrade, alive and well, brought me to a fully sober condition in one second flat! It appeared that whilst strafing what he considered to be the enemy's officers Mess from across the airfield, he touched the ground with his propeller, which disintegrated. He skidded across the airfield, coming to a halt just short of the building

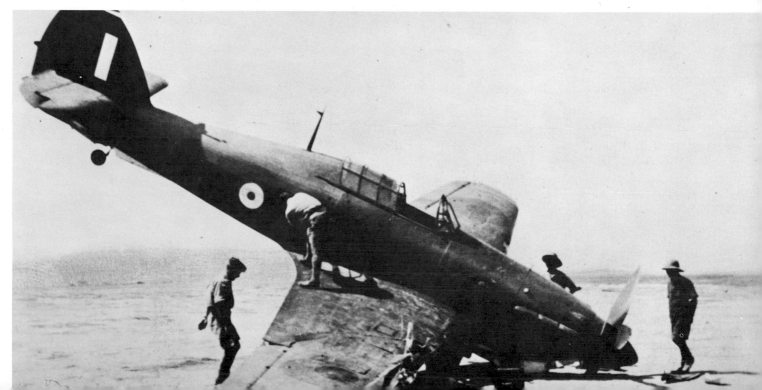

he'd been attacking, and thus quickly changed his status to that of PoW. A very joyful reunion, indeed.

The boredom-cum-nervous tension of standing by ready to 'scramble', kitted up in flying suit and 'Mae West', was interspersed with some moments of extreme excitement which were enjoyed more in retrospect than at the moment of happening. One such occasion was an intended arrival, exactly at dawn, over a railway line in Sicily which was considered important enough to be attacked frequently. I was one of four pilots due to take off 20 minutes before dawn from Luqa. Unfortunately, the armourers bombing up my Hurricane found a technical snag, and it was almost dawn by the time I was able to take off, the other three being long gone. As I was more than half asleep, I suppose I must have expected the same to apply in Sicily, for after dropping my little load and strafing the railway target, and on gaining height again, our wonderful and normally unflappable controller, 'Woody' Woodhall, was almost screaming over the newly-fitted VHF radio for me to get home 'without delay'. I believe the plot on our radar showed something like 170 enemy aircraft airborne and headed for Malta, but the tone of our controller was sufficient to cause another throttle lever to be 'bent'. Being winter, there was a reasonable cloud cover which I used thankfully, but disliking instrument flying and wishing to see if I was nearing the island after some time in cloud, I descended—and found a Macchi 200 on my left and very close!

Indeed, he was close enough for me to see that the pilot was wearing white goggles and had his cockpit closed. A little further away to my right was another Macchi. I don't believe either of them noticed the 'intruder' in their formation, and I was back up into cloud and changing course in a jiffy. All my ammunition had been used in strafing, and I blessed the Italian pilots' poor airmanship for possibly saving my life.

A completely clear field of vision through 360 degrees was, I believe, only second in importance to having a good and thoroughly reliable aircraft, and although slower than one would have wished, our Hurricanes were certainly reliable. A minute or two after veering away from the Macchis, I cautiously broke cloud cover again. No enemy visible, so I nipped down to sea level, over the coast at just above rooftop height and straight into land without the formality of a circuit at Ta Kali. After a tail-up, high-speed spot of taxying to the nearest slit trench and head down, I felt able to breathe again and waited for the strafing to stop.

Although superbly manoeuvrable despite slightly heavy controls, we had to admit reluctantly that the Hurricane did lack speed, but I don't think I ever heard a word spoken against the aircraft. Somehow one loved the Hurricane without either realising or expressing it, and it was only after flying Spitfires with controls light enough for a five year old to handle that one came to realise the strength required to throw a Hurricane about the sky.

Landing on the rock surface, interlaced with stone walls and buildings, was never an easy prospect for the Malta pilots. One casualty (an overshoot) was Z4356, thought to be a 261 Squadron machine.

I joined 6 Squadron on June 22nd, 1942 at its base camp at RAF Shandur on the Suez Canal. I'd recently been promoted to substantive Squadron Leader as an instructor in South Africa and, being 'surplus to requirements', had been posted to the Middle East under a two-way exchange scheme. AHQ selected me for the post of second-in-command of 6 Squadron, under Wing Commander Roger C. Porteus, who was an old friend of mine from Army Co-operation days. By that date the squadron had already been in operations with its Hurricane IIDs during the latter part of the 8th Army's retreat to the El Alamein line, and were presently based at Landing Ground (LG) 91 in the desert west of Alexandria. The Hurricane IID was, at that time, a secret weapon. It was in fact a Hurricane II fitted with two Vickers 'S' guns of 40mm calibre, slung one under each wing, and two .303 inch machine guns. It was created for the prime role of tank destruction from the air because our own tanks were under-gunned compared with the Germans and invariably came off second-best in a tank-versus-tank engagement. The 'S' gun was (with one exception) the biggest calibre weapon to be carried in any RAF aircraft, and the Hurricane had been found to be the best aerial platform upon which to mount it.

Tank-Busters
D. WESTON-BURT

Working up. A 6 Squadron Hurricane IId during the unit's training period at Shandur, 1942.

It had (as I recall) 20 rounds per gun contained in drums. They were armour piercing and designed to break up into fragments on emerging inside the tank, so as to achieve as much damage as possible to the tank's intestines and the crew. The guns were mounted parallel to the fore and aft axis of the aircraft, unlike a fighter which had the guns set to fire four degrees upwards to enable it to get under its prey from behind. The IID, which made its attack at very low level, could not therefore (in theory . . .) fly into the ground, whereas a fighter would, if the gunsight were kept on the target. The rounds could be fired in a burst but this so depressed the nose that in practice they were fired in single pairs, bringing the gunsight back on to target for each pair. It took not much more than half a second to get each pair away.

Training on the type was carried out at Shandur on a captured German tank located in an isolated piece of desert. The attack was started from something like 5,000 feet, putting the aircraft into a dive to achieve 254mph, which with full throttle could be maintained during the

run-in at about 20–40 feet above the ground. Opening with the first pair at about 1,000 yards, two more pairs could be got away accurately before breaking off the attack. It is no exaggeration to say that any good pilot would guarantee to hit his target with one or more pairs on each attack. The tank had little chance of retaliation. Many were equipped with one external machine gun fired from the open turret, but it took a brave man to fire at a Hurricane screaming in at 254mph with two machine guns blazing and a slow crack, crack, crack from its big guns. Normally they battened down and took their punishment. Later in the campaign they dug a slit trench at the side of the tank when stationary and mounted the machine gun vertically in the trench. As the Hurricanes came over, the gunner kept his finger on the trigger, sending a stream of bullets straight up into the air. This was not as dangerous as it might sound, as the aircraft would collect only one or two rounds, but a bullet in the glycol could bring the aircraft down, and once we knew about the trick we made a point of banking away just before the tank.

The two Flight commanders at that stage were Pip Hillier and Julian Walford. Pip Hillier had put up a score of about nine tanks hit and destroyed or put out of action during the retreat. The fitters used to paint a small tank silhouette alongside the cockpit for each tank claimed. Claims were largely unofficial, unlike those of fighter pilots, due to the difficulty of assessing the damage done to the tank or, indeed, how many pilots may have hit the same tank, but later it was fairly reliably assumed that the squadron had destroyed the equivalent of two panzer brigades, which was all there were in the desert, the 19th and 21st. Unfortunately, during a demonstration laid on for the benefit of senior army officers against our tame tank on September 6th, 1942, Pip Hillier banked away too steeply at the end of an attack, did a high speed stall and was killed. Julian Walford, doing searchlight co-operation with the army over Suez on the night of October 2nd, 1942, was blinded by the concentration of light and crashed into an Arab encampment in Sinai. I had done some searchlight co-operation the night before and realised the danger

Above. Splendid underview of a 'tank-killer', fitted with faired Vickers 'S' guns.

Above left: Tank-buster. Z2326, originally built as a Mk II, but converted to become the Mark IV prototype. Fitted here with twin, unfaired 40mm Vickers 'S' cannons.

Left: Can-openers. Close-up view of the sharp end of the twin Vickers 'S' 40mm cannons, so effective against German panzers in the desert war. An aircraft of 6 Squadron, taken possibly at Shandur, 1942

103

Big Stuff. 'Shiny Six' (6 Squadron's Service soubriquet) puts up a foursome for the benefit of the press, 1942. First two aircraft nearest camera are BP188, 'JV-Z, and BP131.

without screens fitted to the fuselage beside the cockpit. I was called up to the advanced landing ground and left Walford in charge of the base camp, and on departure I advised him not to undertake any more co-operation, but he ignored my advice.

I had joined the operational squadron, now on LG89, on July 22nd and had participated in a number of operations, but these were not very notable. One of the first principles of tank-busting was to catch the enemy tanks in the open, away from their second echelon, the backing-up vehicles and defensive anti-aircraft armament. They were then at our mercy, but this state of affairs did not occur often during the preparatory stage leading to the battle of El Alamein. We were forbidden to endanger the valuable aircraft by attacking targets other than tanks and it was wasteful of the heavy ammunition to use it against thin-skinned vehicles. The wisdom of this was brought home to me one day when returning from an abortive sortie, alone except for my No 2, I saw a lone lorry in open country with sandstone hills rising on either side. I came down and gave it a burst with the small guns but in return got a burst of machine gun fire from a gun ensconced in the hills to the right. There was no real damage to my aircraft, but one round hit the armour plating behind my back, and although it could not possibly have hurt me I developed an

induced pain at the spot where the bullet struck.

The battle of El Alamein was heralded at 11.00 hours on the night of October 23rd, 1942 by the largest artillery barrage the world had ever known. From our airfields we could see the whole western horizon lit by thousands of gun flashes. The following morning I was sent off with six Hurricane IIDs on a target of 15 tanks and two half-tracks. We found them, attacked and did considerable damage. I personally claimed three tanks definitely hit. Again, on the 28th, I led six IIDs against a reported target of 15 tanks but on arrival at the map reference could find no tanks. However, as we had come down to ground level for a possible attack, we did fire at anything in sight and my log book tells me that I claimed an ambulance set on fire and a lorry. On November 1st we went out looking for four reported tanks but were recalled in mid-air. On November 3rd we were let loose along with all the other squadrons to play as much havoc as possible with the now retreating German and Italian forces. Again, my logbook states that I claimed four mechanical transports hit (two flamers) and two tanks. I also recall one bus which spewed forth several dozen Italians which we gleefully and callously mowed down as they ran for their lives across the coverless desert. The German forces were by then in full retreat and the Italians, who chivalrously allowed the Germans to take their transport, were to a large extent happily captured. In early December, 6 Squadron was brought back to Edcu, east of Alexandria, and issued with a number of Hurricane IICs in addition to their IIDs and given an additional role of convoy patrolling.

On Christmas Day, following tradition, the officers moved down to the airmen's Mess to serve them their Christmas lunch. The air liaison officer, a major, picked up a number of young pilots in a Jeep, with which he proceeded to do tight turns on the sand airfield. Being naturally top-heavy, the Jeep turned over and the major was killed, while one of the pilots suffered a broken jaw. At about this time I inadvertently hit a tram standard in Alexandria one night with my staff car and suffered some slight concussion. The medical authorities would not let me fly again without a medical check at the general hospital at Heliopolis, outside Cairo, so on January 21st, 1943 I got into a Hurricane IID, flew to Heliopolis, got checked out and flew back 'fit for flying duties . . .' It was perhaps only possible to do this because I was now commanding officer of 6 Squadron, Roger Porteus having been posted to the Staff College in Palestine. I was not to see him again. Years later I was at an airfield in occupied Germany on a special mission. There was to be a dance that night and guests were arriving by air and road. We heard in the Mess that a DH Vampire had crashed on its approach, killing the pilot. Shortly afterwards the news came that it was Wing Commander Porteus.

On February 22nd, 1943 the squadron was moved westward to Bu Amud, equipped still with IIDs and IICs for convoy patrol duties. At that time the convoys through the Mediterranean were liable to be harassed by German U-boats and some ships were being sunk. Our task was to try to spot the U-boats from above, radio for assistance and in the meantime endeavour to distract the U-boat with some small bombs we carried. There was also the chance of Italian long range small bombers trying their luck, and an incident occurred on February 15th which might bear recounting. The early warning radar chaps in our area had detected blips in the early morning indicating that enemy aircraft were penetrating close to the coast, obviously on anti-shipping sweeps. They suggested that we put up two aircraft before dawn to hang around and wait for them. I took a No 2 with me and patrolled for four and a half hours in rather cloudy conditions until, about to give up, I came down to sea level and saw, also skimming the waves, two Savoia SM79s. We gave chase but they were a match for us in speed. We were flying IIDs and I called up my No 2 to try lobbing the big shells at them. We tried this for a bit with no obvious success and then, consulting my fuel gauges, I realised we had little enough fuel to get us home. I turned and headed for base gaining height slowly and in due course landed with one and half gallons in the tanks. The following day an enemy aircraft was reported in the water and I was told that I would be credited with the kill, but I never had any confirmation. The squadron was now instructed to move from Bu Amud to Castel Benito in Libya, and the move was made on March 3rd, 1943, the aircraft flying up in one day, leaving the ground crews to follow by road. On arrival there seemed to be some slight misunderstanding somewhere, and there was no space for us. However, we were quickly found an airfield called Sorman on the coast. We were now back in our proper role of tank buster and were being brought in to assist in the coming difficult battles envisaged in the vicinity of Gabes, where the mountains would assist Rommel in making a stand.

For some many weeks prior to this, General Le Clerc of the Free French had been leading a force of around 200 white and 2,000 native troops across the Sahara from the vicinity of Lake Chad. It was known as the Lake Chad Expedition. It was not all that formidable as a force, being armed mostly with small arms and machine guns, but nevertheless it was a creditable effort on the part of the Free French to assist in the campaign. On arrival south of the mountains near Gabes, General Le Clerc was asked to establish his camp there and to use his men to prepare a route which General Montgomery could utilise in one of his now-famous outflanking movements, skirting the mountains and returning to the coast to the west of Gabes and, with luck, bottling up a proportion of Rommel's army. The Germans discovered the presence of this French force south of their positions and despatched a strong armoured column of tanks, armoured cars and supply vehicles, possibly 50 in total, to round up the French and bring them in. However, the 8th Army, on the 'Y' Intercept, became aware of the German plan and called on the RAF to intervene. This was a job for 6 Squadron.

On March 10th we were called up to a small advanced LG known as Hasbub Satellite. We could muster 19 Hurricane IIDs and pilots. On arrival we landed and dispersed the aircraft in the open, and soon discovered that we were under shell-fire from some heavy guns located high in the mountains to the south-west. We huddled behind some sand dunes where we found a solitary RAF wireless operator and his equipment. After a while our group commander, Group Captain Atcherley flew in, joined us behind the sand dunes and brought us up to date on events. Apparently a SAAF reconnaissance squadron was sending out sorties to try to locate the German column, but had so far failed to do so. As the day drew on, with no new developments, I suggested to Group Captain Atcherley that, as I was an ex-Army co-operation pilot, I had as good a chance as the recce pilots of finding the German column. He agreed and sent out a call for two squadrons of Spitfires as cover to escort us. When these appeared in the sky, we took off, 13 of us for the first attack, leaving six in reserve. I headed south to the extent of the German lines, turned west and then north again behind the German lines.

At the position where the column was reported to be I looked down and, with considerable surprise, saw them almost immediately beneath us. We were not in a good position to attack. We liked to espy our target from some distance, dive and come in at very low level hoping to achieve some measure of surprise. As we had been seen I decided to go straight down into the attack, and in so doing received a large shell in my port wing. I did not know until then that in diving straight at a gun firing towards one, one could see the shells coming up. For some five minutes we flew to and fro across the column, dealing out savage destruction. Each time a tank went on fire there were shouts of exultation over the R/T. When I thought we must have knocked out every tank and vehicle, and having seen none of our aircraft go down, I thought I would not push our luck too far, and called the squadron together and headed for home. The fighter cover, unable to resist the temptation, carried on ground strafing the remnants, and the Group Captain, no doubt hearing it all over the R/T, despatched the remaining six IIDs under my senior Flight commander, Flight Lieutenant Bluett, to give the *coup de grace*. On arrival at base, Sorman, I resisted the impulse to do a low victory roll to indicate to those on the ground the success of our mission. It was as well that I did, because after landing I found I had a nine inch hole in the ten inch main spar of my left wing . . .! We subsequently learned that General Le Clerc was able to witness the whole attack from his entrenched position, and a very relieved officer he must have been. He decided to give the *Croix de*

Guerre to the three squadron leaders of the first wave and Flight Lieutenant Bluett. The Germans sent out tank recovery vehicles and removed some of the tanks, but a ground reconnaissance proved that our claims of almost complete destruction of the column were no exaggeration.

By March 22nd the Allied forces were well advanced in their outflanking movement but had come up against resistance from the Germans, including the 21st Panzer brigade, and 6 Squadron was called upon. We found the tanks facing each other in fairly open country and attacked, making several passes to and fro. We inflicted considerable damage. I recall one pilot flying straight over his victim and receiving a hunk of tank in the underbelly of his aircraft. Having returned to base we were sent out again on the same target as soon as we had refuelled and rearmed. On March 24th we did a sortie but it could not have been of much import as my log book merely records, 'hit in Browning' and 'Sgt Harris killed near El Hamma'. Which leads me to digress

slightly regarding Sergeant Harris. He was a very young newcomer to the squadron and on his first operation he was hit by anti-aircraft fire and had to land wheels-up in the desert. This was not a particularly unusual occurrence, and when his turn came up he went on his second operation. Again he was hit, landed and returned safely to the squadron. This must have been enough to shake any man's morale and I realised he needed careful handling. I decided to let him do one more operational flight and, assuming he returned safely, to recommend he be stood down for a while. However this time he was shot down and killed. I felt he had well deserved a decoration, but on consulting King's Regulations I discovered that only the Victoria Cross and Mentioned in Despatches could be awarded posthumously. I duly recommended him for an MiD, which was in fact awarded.

The two armies were by now operating in very hilly and even wooded country and it was difficult to get good targets. On April 6th we were out looking for a reported

Briefing. Pilots of 6 Squadron being briefed by the unit commander, Squadron Leader R. Slade-Betts, DSO DFC (far left)—a photo taken late in the war, but wholly representative of hundreds of similar occasions in the desert.

assembly of tanks but in the wooded ravines they had excellent cover and we were subjected to considerable anti-aircraft fire from gun positions we could not see. My particular friend, Flying Officer Zillessen, did not return from this mission, and we assumed him dead. Many weeks later we had news that he was a prisoner of war in Italy. How he got his Hurricane down in one piece in that country I shall probably never know. On April 7th we did an armed reconnaissance which yielded nothing and then we were sent out on what was thought to be an excellent target of tanks in the sandy country near the coast. I had decided that it was about time I allowed my Flight commanders to lead the odd sortie, and had already let Flight Lieutenant Bluett lead one, whilst I led the second six aircraft. This time I instructed my other Flight commander to lead. I led the second six. He proceeded westwards several miles inland of the coast, searching to the north towards the Mediterranean. He saw some tanks and no doubt recognised them as American Shermans, but what he did not notice was that they were proceeding *eastwards* towards our lines. A short distance further on he sighted a conglomeration of vehicles, assumed they were German tanks facing the Shermans, and immediately dived to the attack. What in fact had happened was that the Germans had captured the Shermans from the Americans on the 2nd Army front and brought them down against the 8th Army. We were attacking the second echelon of this force (normally we never attacked tanks unless they were divorced from their second echelon). As we came in at low level the flak came to meet us. We crossed slightly in front of the second echelon of tanks so that the flak came from our port side. The leading aircraft flew straight through it. Being behind and hugging the ground, I realised there was no chance of getting through this murderous curtain of fire. There were tracers in the belts, so that it was possible to see the direction and concentration of the flak. It was impossible to get under it and suicidal to fly through it.

There was only one chance. I kept my Flight low on the deck until we were about to enter the worst of the flak. Then,

pulling back hard on the stick, I lifted the aircraft over it, hoping the others would follow suit. I then headed at full throttle out to sea. There was no sign of any of the rest of the squadron so I returned cautiously to land. I saw one of my aircraft, a ball of fire as a result of the fuselage tank having gone up, slowly fly into the ground and explode. I could find no others and returned to base. To add insult to injury, a British army gunner had a go at me as I flew over his position.

Only six of us came back by air. Three walked in later, but three had been killed, Flying Officers Walter and Clarke and Sergeant Hastings. This was our most tragic mission. Since El Alamein we had lost only six pilots killed and one captured, and three had gone on this one operation. Admittedly we had been incorrectly briefed. We were told to expect German Tiger tanks, but the real cause of the failure was inexperience on the part of the leader, and foolhardy courage in leading his squadron into a dangerous position Shortly after this I was posted to a Kittyhawk Wing, with a view to taking it over, but that is another story. Apparently I was staying alive too long and holding up promotion in the squadron . . .

Left: Unusual view of the tank-busting Hurricane's armament. Jacked and (necessarily) braced, this aircraft was about to have its Vickers 'S' guns butt-tested.

Below left/below: At the receiving end—two views of a German tank which was devastated by the pin-point accuracy of a pair of Vickers 'S' cannons — just one of 6 Squadron's many victims.

109

Alamein by Night
GRAHAM LEGGETT

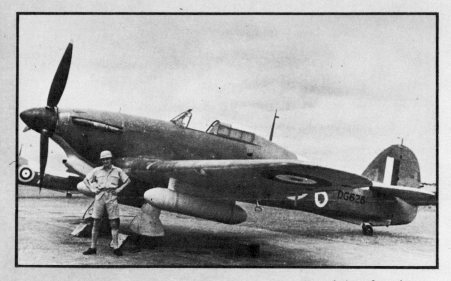

DG626, a Hurricane IId, marked '6' on fuselage, awaiting a delivery flight from Takoradi, late 1941 or early 1942. Standing by its nose is Sergeant L. Davies.

Supplies of aircraft to the DAF came (necessarily) by a long and tortuous route via West Africa for much of the time. One central 'depot' which received them from England, built and serviced, and then flew delivery flights clear across the African continent, was established at Takoradi. This equivalent of an RAF Maintenance Unit was (literally) hacked out of an equatorial jungle and soon became the major focal half-way stage for the DAF's re-equipment. In this view a line of Hurricanes is being fuelled (the hard way . . .) in preparation for a delivery shuttle flight. Second from left is BE715 which served with 250 Squadron in mid-1942.

Above: TAC-R. The value of tactical reconnaissance was first shown vividly during the early stages of the North African campaign. On-the-spot development of the photos brought back by roving Tac-R Hurricanes was necessary if results were to be of any help to local commanders. One 'instant' developing 'dark room' is seen here.

Right: The Desert Air Force (DAF) was composed literally of every Allied nationality to take part in the war. Such a conglomeration of languages, creeds and widely-differing backgrounds amalgamated astonishingly well in the desert 'team'. Here, two aircraft of 237 (Rhodesian) Squadron are taking-off, May 12th, 1942.

On October 27th, 1942, for the fifth night in succession, the western skyline was ablaze with the flashes of a thousand guns, their thunder trembling through the ground to set the cocoa mugs chattering on the table of 73 Squadron's pilots' Mess tent. Earlier that evening the pilots had flown their black-painted Hurricane IICs from their desert strip south-west of Alexandria to the advanced landing ground (ALG) at Burg-el-Arab (sometimes known as 'Bugger-the-wog' . . .). Then at dusk the first aircraft had taken off on a night-long programme of individual sorties where planning, stealth and precision meant the difference between success and disaster. All our pilots were experienced; mostly from day-fighter squadrons. Some had fought over Malta, others had hunted Germans in the night skies of Britain, a couple had been flying instructors. Now together they formed one of the most un-usual Hurricane squadrons of the war—hitting the enemy behind his lines at night

and keeping the Luftwaffe away from ours. Many an Afrika Korps driver, feeling safe on a dark road miles from the fighting front, had been hit from apparently nowhere by the four 20mm cannons of these night prowlers. But on this night the essential task was to prevent the enemy aircraft from attacking the 8th Army, to which end the squadron was to maintain standing patrols over the battle zone. The turning point at the north end of our patrol lines was a tiny village, then unknown, called El Alamein.

Even under the light of a bright desert moon it required little navigational skill to find one's way to the patrol line. One simply took off, spiralled quickly up to a few thousand feet and then set off along the coast in the direction of the battle. It took only a few minutes to reach El Alamein and the whole incredible scene was set out like a huge illuminated map. To the east and reaching away southwards, the countless guns of the 8th Army kept up

Bottom left: Aussie Hurris. Line up of 451 Squadron RAAF, nearest machine being Z4036.

One of the more daring operations of the desert air war was the four-days 'detachment' of No 243 Wing (213 and 238 Squadrons), led by the legendary Wing Commander Johnny Darwen, DSO, DFC, November 13th to 16th, 1942. A total of 36 Hurricanes, supported by Lockheed Hudson transports, were established secretly on a bald landing area, some 140 miles *behind* the Axis front lines, titled Landing Ground (LG) 125. The object was to harass retreating Axis ground forces along the Libyan coastal strip, following the successful battle of El Alamein. In four short days the Wing destroyed or knocked out of action over 300 vehicles (and their human contents), 15 aircraft on the ground and two more in the air—all for the loss of three Hurricanes missing in action, plus four more abandoned on return to 'friendly' territory. Seen here is a 213 Squadron Hurricane IIc, HL887, AK-W, with one of the Hudsons which 'lifted' supplies and personnel to and from LG125.

Right: Pick-up. Captain K. A. Quirk, SAAF, who on May 16th, 1941 landed behind the enemy lines to help a squadron comrade, Lieutenant Burger, who had been forced down. Sitting on Burger's knees, Quirk took off again and flew back to base (as illustrated here). Quirk was later awarded a DSO for this the first of many such 'two-some' rescues by fighter pilots throughout the desert campaign. *Babs*, painted on the cockpit panel, was Quirk's pet name for his wife.

their relentless barrage of fire, flash following flash so closely that the surrounding terrain stood out in sharp relief, betraying positions and emplacements. From the west came the replying fire of enemy guns, less numerous perhaps, but nonetheless insistent. And among the positions of both sides, which at places was impossible to divide, the sudden flash of bursting shells of every calibre, gleaming briefly through the dust clouds. Nor in the night did the enemy find relief from his hammering from the air for, like great smoky candles in the sky, parachute flares drifted slowly downwards upon his lines, adding more light to the scene and enabling our night bombers to pile even more discomfort upon the men beneath. Not that the enemy was taking it lying down—red and green tracers arched upwards and amongst the fluffy white clouds heavy AA shells flicker and puffed.

From the snugness of my cockpit, with the instruments glowing softly, a voiceless R/T hissing in the earphones and the contented roar of the Merlin drowning all other sound, it was difficult to imagine what was really happening down there on

Far left: Spaghetti Paint. A 3 Squadron RAAF Hurricane at Benina airfield in 1941, with unusual 'camouflage' markings applied to its nose and wing leading edges, fairly similar to the contemporary Italian camouflage paint schemes.

Left: The desert was not always 'burning sands'. 32 Squadron's Hurricanes, seen on Maison Blanche airstrip in early 1943, could vouch for the 'English weather' often encountered in North Africa.

Below left: No 94 Squadron, based at El Gamil in late 1942, was equipped with Hurricane IIc four 20mm cannon versions. Included were three of four presentation Hurricanes, paid for by Lady MacRobert in memory of her three sons—all killed whilst flying. All three aircraft are seen here. From front: BP389 (GO-C); BP387 (GO-J); HL851 (GO-P, *Sir Roderic*); HL735 (*Sir Iain*); HL844 (*Sir Alasdair*). The fourth MacRobert Hurricane was titled *MacRobert's Salute to Russia*; whilst earlier Lady MacRobert had 'presented' a Short Stirling bomber to the RAF—*MacRobert's Reply*. In this view the Hurricanes are fitted with two cannons only, in the interests of better performance.

115

Above: Off to the war. Z4769, '3' en route to the Middle East operational theatre from Takoradi, August 1941.

Top: Greek warrior. HW798, AK-P, of 213 Squadron, pictured at Paphos, Greece, in September 1943. Note the medium-range 'cigar' petrol tanks fitted externally under the wings.

Right: LF498, a Hurricane Mk IV of 6 Squadron, landing at Tatoi, Greece in late 1944. This aircraft destroyed a rail bridge at Spuz 'single-handed' with a rocket attack in November 1944, during the Balkan campaign.

the battlefield. On occasion men on the ground have spoken with admiration of those who fought their war in the air. What is seldom realised, however, is the sense of detachment with which most airmen went about their business. A target was simply a target, be it an iron-crossed aircraft, a ship at sea, a truck in the desert or a pinpoint on the ground. Rarely does an airman catch more than a glimpse of other humans manning such targets, and hardly ever does he witness the remains of his comrades or those he has destroyed. So it was with a sense of unreality that I watched history being made in this wilderness of rock and sand—so aptly described as a place only fit for war.

During that crucial night, enemy air activity seemed to be minimal. It was not until my tanks were emptying and my relief already on his way that the R/T provided news that a 'bandit' was about. Suddenly it was my war again. Hood open to improve visibility—check gunsights—increase revs—tighten straps—search the night sky. But then control called my

Above: Mixed load. A Hurricane with four 3 inch RP under one wing, and a medium-range fuel tank under the other, belonging to the Balkan Air Force, taxies out for take-off in Greece, watched by a gaggle of Spitfire pilots.

Left: West African Defender. A Hurricane of 128 Squadron, sporting a red/white/blue spinner, being serviced at Hastings, Sierra Leone—a unit formed specifically for defence of the Allied ports and bases in West Africa, and commanded initially by Squadron Leader Billy Drake, DSO DFC, a veteran of the desert air war in which he commanded 112 (Shark) Squadron.

117

relieving colleague and proceeded to vector him towards the 'bandit'. My orders —'Pancake'. Reluctantly easing back the throttle, I started to descend, peering along the coastline to identify a point at which to turn inland towards the airstrip. At that moment the cockpit exploded in a blinding sheet of white light! The speed with which the computer brain analyses

alarming rate. Then, as I turned for a second attack, the flare broke up and plunged earthwards, trailing sparks as it went. By then my colleague was chasing the German out to sea, but the night's adventure was not quite over for, still dazzled, seeing detail on the ground was most difficult. With tanks running dry I finally found the marker flares and then searched feverishly for the tiny glim lights of the flare path. Then, with remaining flying time reduced to bare minutes, and visions of a belly landing coming closer, a double red Very light soared upwards a few miles eastwards. God bless our vigilant OC Night Flying..! Within moments I had completed final actions and settled the wheels rather firmly on the sand. Taxying in, I was happy to find my night vision beginning to return. To the west the horizon continued to flicker into the night and I reflected on the spectacle I had just observed from a grand-stand seat. For myself, for a few hours at least, the war was less immediate, and on pulling back the flap of the intelligence officer's tent, I answered his questioning glance with my report—a 'flamer'.

Above: Big Lift. Using a Coles crane, an R & SU party swings the fuselage of BD930, from 73 Squadron, on to the trailer of a 'Queen—Mary'. The squadron insignia comprised a central yellow 'dart', bordered by two blue.

Right: Delta Convoy. Three battle-damaged Hurricanes aboard 'Queen Mary' transporters en route to a Maintenance Unit south of Cairo, near the Tura foothills. In background can be seen two of the well-known Gizeh Pyramids. Nearest Hurricane is Z4967, 'D' of 229 Squadron.

Top centre: The state of some salvaged aircraft was so bad that a new maintenance 'instruction' was jokingly introduced by the indefatigable ground crews—'Item 1. Sit fresh pilot in middle of dispersal and commence building aircraft around him...!' A typical scene was this view of a repair gang at work at Maison Blanche airfield, Algiers.

such moments is remarkable. In a split second it compares all known facts, examines technical data and proceeds to supply answers. Surely an AA shell? But at such close range, why no apparent damage to me or my machine? Then I realised I could see very little except for a very bright white light, reflected, as I then realised, in the rear-view mirror. Banking gently into a turn, I could focus upon it more easily—a parachute flare. It must have burst immediately over my cockpit, presumably having been dropped by the reported 'bandit'—who, in this light, must surely be visible. Holding the Hurricane in a series of 360 degree turns, I scoured the night sky. But with my night vision temporarily (I hoped . . .) impaired, I could see nothing except the glare of the flare—which, incidentally, our troops on the ground would not be feeling too happy about.

I soon discovered that ranging on a flare was not especially easy. It tends to hang motionless at a considerable distance, and then rush into the gunsight at an

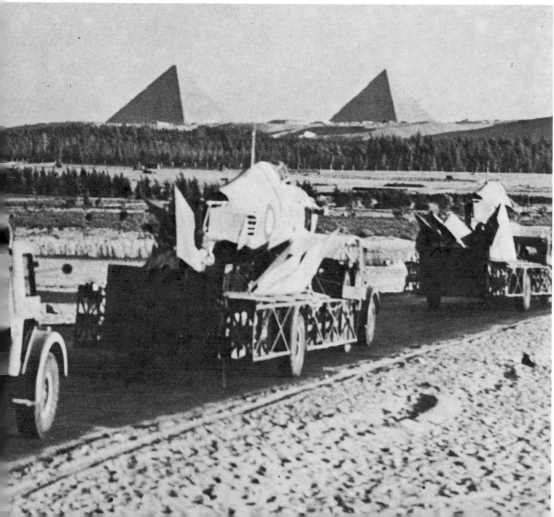

Above: Repair and Salvage. A substantial contribution to the DAF's final superiority in the air over the desert war was made by the unpublicised R & SUs—the Repair and Salvage Units of the RAF. Living away from any 'base' airfield for weeks at a time, these parties of ground crew literally scoured the sands for crashed aircraft and brought them back for reclamation, repair and re-issue to the front-line units. A measure of their tremendous effort is the fact that in one four month period alone, they recovered just over 1,000 crashed aircraft, and were able to send some 800 of these back into battle. A typical 'scavenging crew' is seen here on its way to the Allied back areas with its latest 'collection' of salvageable Hurricanes, strapped on the trailers of their 'Queen Mary' lorries, and stopping for a traditional 100-mile brew-up. The mixture of parent units of the aircraft is evident from the various code letters.

Hurricane pilots who were employed in the day fighter role, and had the necessary night flying experience, were frequently called upon to undertake missions which were outside the normal span of daylight operations and which, later, were more appropriately allocated to the night, all-weather fighters equipped with sophisticated airborne radar and a second crew member employed as a radar operator. Thus, although never officially designated a night fighter pilot nor specifically trained as such, I was often called upon, in common with other 'suitably qualified' day fighter pilots, to fly Hurricane sorties either in darkness to augment the night fighter forces, or in the grey hours of dawn or dusk which could not readily be defined as belonging exclusively to day or night fighters. These missions varied widely in character but not in probability of success. Although few were prepared to admit it at the time, it is clear (in retrospect) that the odds against any tangible success were extremely high. Nevertheless, there is some evidence to suggest that the very presence of fighters, whether day or night, patrolling over likely targets or being directed on to

Vigil by night. A Hurricane stands ready for a night patrol. The pilot's flying helmet is 'hung' over the gunsight—a fitter carries out final cockpit checks.

Night Fighters
G. A. BROWN

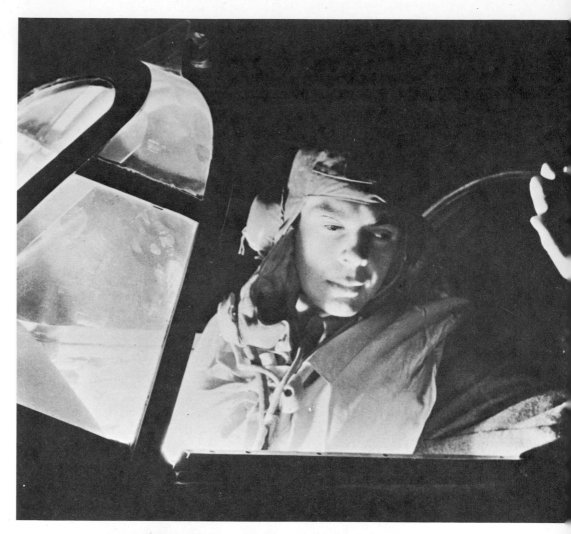

Right: Chocks Gone. A night fighter pilot gives a wave of the hand to acknowledge the ground crew's call and prepares to taxi. Cockpit lighting is on full here, but will be subdued within a few seconds.

Right: Night Stalkers. Pilots of 85 Squadron relax in the Readiness hut, prior to another night's work, their eyes protected by 'dimmer' glasses in order to assist their night vision. Second from right is the squadron commander, Squadron Leader Peter Townsend, DFC, with his pet Alsatian 'Kim'.

enemy aircraft, acted as a deterrent and possibly resulted in the otherwise unexplained jettisoning of lethal bomb loads on open ground or in the sea, or in raiders turning for home before reaching their targets and discharging their bombs.

My lasting impression of my own night fighter activities is one of utter impotence and frustration, arising from my abject failure ever to see anything of the enemy except perhaps, a fleeting glimpse of the shadowy form of an aircraft hurrying across my flight path, or flashing past in the opposite direction. In either event one was faced with the awful choice between, on the one hand, trying to guess the right course to steer to re-establish contact, followed by a long and probably futile chase; and on the other hand, ignoring the sighting and hoping for another contact giving a more favourable attacking position. The sad truth is that the accuracy of the ground control organisation, which proved reasonably adequate for daylight interception in conditions of average visibility, was not of a sufficiently high order in darkness or poor visibility to ensure that the single-seater fighter pilot, with no airborne radar and only one pair of eyes at his disposal, would be brought into visual contact with his quarry or, if he was, that he would be in a viable position to lainch an attack. In average visibility

by day the pilot's position in relation to the target when he made visual contact was not nearly so critical as it was in poor visibility or darkness. Generally speaking, if he had superiority in height and/or speed and was not put on a head-on collision course with the target, the day fighter pilot would be quite happy and capable of manoeuvring himself into the most advantageous attacking position. Visual contact in the shortest possible time was the main ingredient of a good daylight fighter interception. Assuming the normal speed superiority of the fighter over a bomber, relative course was of secondary importance. By these criteria, ground controllers could claim a fair measure of success in daylight operations. But there is at least a suspicion that they used the same criteria by night whereas, of course, speed of interception and visual contact were meaningless aims unless the fighter was in a position to launch his attack without losing that all-important visual contact.

There is also reason to believe that the controllers, accustomed to day fighter pilots reporting sightings of aircraft at great distances in daylight, over-estimated the visual acuity of a pilot's eye in darkness. It was possible for a pilot to improve his visual efficiency at night insofar as he could train himself to search the sky

The pause before opening up to full power for take-off. Wing tip lights on, the pilot's cockpit thrown into sharp relief by a background searchlight along the runway, a night owl is about to make its run.

Airborne. A Hurricane IIc, PZ869 starts its climb towards its patrol area.

systematically and thus improve his chances of acquiring a target. There were those who, like John Cunningham (known as 'Cat's Eyes'), had perfected their night visual capability to a high degree and achieved remarkable success in night fighter operations, even managing to bring off the occasional freelance interception. But I am still convinced that these successes owed more to an uncanny instinct or sixth sense than to any extraordinary physical attribute, and the claim by journalists and others that a diet of carrots or special vitamins was beneficial to night vision was entirely fanciful. In summary, until the advent of GCI (Ground Control Interception) radar and airborne radar, fighter control, relying as it did on early warning radar and Royal Observer Corps reporting, was just not accurate enough in darkness or poor visibility to give a pilot more than an outside chance of successful interception and attack.

Perhaps in recognition of the limitations of close control from the ground, we Hurricane pilots were only rarely scrambled at night to intercept or investigate specific targets. Even so, these sorties proved all too often to be completely

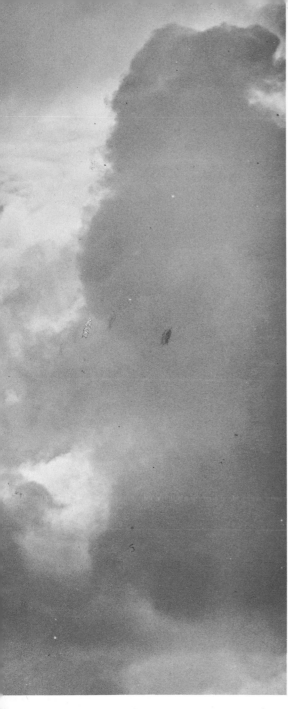

abortive, with the plots themselves sometimes fading mysteriously whilst we were ostensibly in full pursuit of a quarry. On one such notable occasion, after using most of my fuel chasing an alleged hostile plot, I was informed apologetically by ground control that the source of the plot reported by the ROC had in fact been identified as an army lorry manoeuvring in the area! Thereafter, whenever we were scrambled on what we suspected to be a false errand, the catch-phrase 'Sorry, lorry' was yelled in chorus by all in the crew room . . .

More usually, we were employed in a freelance role on standing area or line patrols covering vulnerable targets such as major towns and cities, bomber bases or other military installations and, occasionally, sea convoys. On this type of mission we were under a very loose form of control from the ground, receiving only snippets of information from time to time about hostile movements in our area. Otherwise, we were left very much to our own devices, initiative, instinct and, perhaps most of all, to the whims of pure chance. There were several variations of the standing patrol, some involving integration between day fighters and AA guns, or night fighters, or both. I recall one such night operation in particular which was mounted during a fairly heavy bomber raid over Sheffield. On this occasion Defiants and Hurricanes were 'stepped' upwards at 500 feet intervals from 12,000 feet, below which the AA guns were given freedom of action, I was allocated a height band of 18,000 feet with the Defiants patrolling below. An esti-

Suez Defence. Soot-black Hurricanes of 213 Squadron revving in unison during 1941, when the unit was charged with the defence of the Suez Canal area in Egypt. Based (ostensibly) at Nicosia, Cyprus, the unit was split into several detached Flights along the Canal area and in Cyprus— the Flight pictured here being (it is believed) at Ismailia, Egypt.

mated 20-plus bombers were reported over Sheffield at the time and the effects of their attack were clearly visible and most spectacular. There were many fires caused by incendiary and high explosive bombs providing a brilliant back-cloth against which aircraft were occasionally silhouetted Yet, even in these seemingly ideal conditions contact was so fleeting that positive identification was virtually impossible and pursuit futile. The strange thing was that, with three fighter squadrons operating over Sheffield that night in better than normal visibility because of the ground conflagrations, not one successful engagement was reported. Perhaps there is some consolation in the fact that, with collision more than a remote possibility, all our fighter aircraft reported safely to base, but our inability to provide Sheffield with any respite from the bombing, or restitution against the bombers was extremely frustrating and saddening.

On another occasion I was scrambled on a dark night with Squadron Leader (later, Air Marshal Sir) David Atcherley to patrol Hull, which was being subjected to sporadic attacks by German bombers. Again, we were given freedom of action above 12,000 feet with the AA guns operating below that height. There was comprehensive searchlight cover in the area and we were hoping for some successful co-operation with them. We were able to observe fairly frequent bomb bursts on the ground and heavy AA response, but in spite of intense searchlight activity, we never saw a single German bomber illuminated by them. Eventually David Atcherley asked for authority to reduce height so that we could operate where we judged the German bombers to be flying, approximately at 8,000 feet. This authority was given after the guns were silenced, but immediately we descended to this new height we were picked up by the searchlights and relentlessly held by them, although we repeatedly asked our controller to order them to be doused. The glare from the multiple criss-cross of searchlight beams reduced our visibility outside the cockpit to nil and made instrument reading inside the cockpit virtually impossible because of reflection. At last, in desperation, David Atcherley pulled out his trump card. He told the fighter controller that unless every searchlight in the area was immediately doused, he would bail out, and added that although it was impossible accurately to pinpoint his position, he believed he was over the centre of Hull. Needless to say, within five seconds every searchlight within sight was extinguished, leaving an inky blackness which by contrast was even more impenetrable than the glare of the searchlights. With friendly guidance from our controller, however, we returned safely to base after yet another abortive and frustrating night fighter defence sortie.

These accounts, illustrating the limitations of the Hurricane in the night fighter

Touch-down. Squadron Leader Ian Gleed, DFC, OC 87 Squadron, landing his personal Hurricane, P2798, LK-A, at Colerne on February 6th, 1941. Painted overall black, except for his personal nose marking (in pale blue) and rudder striping.

role, do not imply any general criticism of the aeroplane which endeared itself to most fighter pilots as a robust, efficient and viceless fighter, although somewhat lacking in performance as compared with its contemporaries. I flew both Spitfires and Typhoons as well as Hurricanes on fighter defence missions at night, and although the Hurricane, and to a greater extent the Typhoon, were probably potentially better night fighters than the Spitfire (which I preferred as a day fighter), none was really up to the task with the ground environment and airborne equipment then at our disposal. One of the serious limitations of the Hurricane at night was brought home to me when, as a Flight commander, I was scrambled from Martlesham Heath with two pilots from

my Flight to combat a German bomber raid over Ipswich. My instructions were to patrol over the town at about 12,000 feet and, again, on this occasion there was searchlight and AA activity but I was unable to detect any bomb bursts. Needless to say, I saw no other aircraft, friend or foe, and after about an hour I was recalled with perhaps enough fuel for an emergency diversion if necessary. On arrival over base I was told that there was a hostile aircraft lurking in the vicinity and was ordered to provide cover whilst the other two Hurricanes were landed. I was given a couple of tentative courses to steer in the hope that I might pick up the 'bandit' but saw nothing and was then ordered to land, with (by that time) just sufficient fuel for a circuit and perhaps one

Above: Night Intruder. Squadron Leader J. A. F. MacLachlan DSO, DFC, commander of No 1 Squadron RAF during the period it was engaged in night intrusion operations over Occupied Europe. A veteran of Malta and the desert war, 'Mac' had his left arm amputated after being shot down over Malta, but flew with an artificial arm instead. His war total was 17 victories before his death in July 1943.

Above left: *Night Fighter*—a drawing by Eric Kennington, which portrays one of the greatest Hurricane night 'aces', Squadron Leader Richard Playne Stevens, DSO, DFC. He claimed a total of 14 victories by night with 151 Squadron, without the benefit of radar, but was lost in action eventually on December 15th, 1941, whilst serving with 253 Squadron.

overshoot. Almost inevitably (it seemed) as I was making my circuit the airfield controller announced that he had received instructions to extinguish all airfield lighting because of the close proximity of an unidentified aircraft. Thereupon the airfield was plunged into darkness but I had no alternative but to complete my circuit and land as best I could without any form of lighting. Fortunately, I was not restricted to a runway, my circuit pattern was well established by then and I was able to distinguish sufficient features in the final approach to judge my touch-down point. Nevertheless, I was a little apprehensive about the final landing and the

aircraft appeared to spend an unduly long time in a stalled condition before finally reaching the ground with a resounding thud, though with no apparent ill-effects. This episode, although otherwise unproductive, brought home to me the Hurricane's general unsuitability and lack of flexibility in particular in the night fighter role. An aeroplane which could not spend an hour on patrol, including a period of full throttle combat, and still be capable of a diversion hardly deserved serious consideration as a night fighter.

This is certainly not to say that the Hurricane was never used to good effect at night during the war. Indeed, there was

Black Beast. BE500, the personal Hurricane IIc of Squadron Leader Denis Smallwood, commander of 87 Squadron from November 1941 to September 1942. His rank pennant is displayed just below the windscreen.

a small and elite band of extremely skilled and adventurous Hurricane pilots who achieved remarkable success in night intruder operations, attacking and destroying enemy aircraft within their own airfield circuit. These extraordinary and highly individualistic exploits however did nothing to vindicate the Hurricane in the night fighter defence role. Rather did they emphasise the validity of that most fundamental of all military doctrines which asserts that attack is the best form of defence. They also demonstrated how the Hurricane could more profitably have been used to counter Hitler's night offensive against Britain. Where better, in other words, to seek out and attack the enemy raider than over his own base, particularly at night when everything favours the intruder?

Nor is the Hurricane's indifferent record in the night interceptor role any reflection on the calibre and training of the pilots, many of whom went on to make highly successful night fighter pilots when flying suitably equipped multi-seat aeroplanes. In the days of intensive training prior to and after the outbreak of war, night flying was practised regularly and assiduously by all day fighter pilots for, apart from the Blenheim Is which were just assuming the role and, later, Defiants there were no specialised night fighter aircraft. It was in fact generally understood that the single-seat fighters would have to bear the brunt of night fighter defence. One of the most important training exercises then was night formation flying and the more experienced of us also tried simple aerobatic manoeuvres in formation, tail chases and dogfights. Needless to say, all such manoeuvres were carried out with navigation lights burning, but it gave one great confidence in handling the aircraft at night and helped enormously in judging distances, approach speeds, ranging and sighting of guns. Without the benefit of navigation/identification lights, visual acquistion, judgement of closing speeds, sighting and ranging became operations of exceptional skill which few mastered, and only then after much experience and practice. It was also quite hazardous and recognition of the fact is implicit in the popular belief at that time that premature baldness amongst fighter pilots was due to one or other of two nocturnal activities—the more likely being dogfighting at night without navigation lights!

It is a melancholy and, to many, a perplexing thought that the Hurricane which proved such an excellent all-purpose day fighter, and whose effectiveness as a bomber destroyer, especially, had been proved beyond doubt, should have made so little impact on the Luftwaffe's night offensive against Britain. Had the sophisticated ground environment and pilot-operated airborne radar equipment subsequently developed been available then, perhaps quite a different story could have been told.

129

Over the Chindwin.
BP704 of 28 Squadron
patrolling along the
Chindwin River in
Northern Burma, 1943.

Burma Bomber. A
Hurricane IIc (unit
unidentified) on the Arakan
front receiving its ration of
500lb GP bombs, and re-
arming of its four 20mm
cannons.

Jungle Fighters
E. D. C. LEWIS

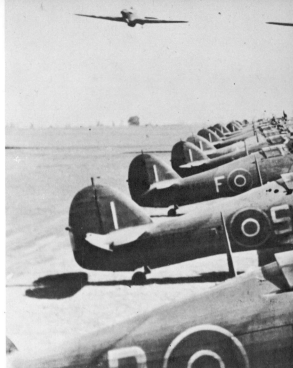

The chronicles of the Hurricane in the Far East theatre of operations deserve a book unto themselves. From the debacle of Singapore in early 1942 until the final defeat of Japan in August 1945, Hurricanes played a leading and vital part in the 'Forgotten War'. Due to vacillation and jingoistic complacency on the part of the contemporary British government and military high command, when the Japanese finally invaded Singapore—that 'impregnable British fortress' as Winston Churchill so naively termed it—a mere handful of Hurricanes (51, mostly crated, and without sufficient trained pilots) were available to spearhead the outmoded RAF fighters stationed there. During the desperate and bitter fighting retreat through Java, Sumatra and Burma to India, driblets of Hurricanes were thrown into the struggle, and lost unnecessarily because of sheer weakness in overall air strength.

The long trail back from the Indian border to final victory owed a not inconsiderable debt to the Hurricanes and their determined crews. By June 1943 a total of 23 squadrons were equipped with Hurricanes, almost exclusively Mark IIs, although a few Mark IVs had just arrived in Ceylon—a total of nearly 700 Hurricanes for the imminent land offensive by the Allies. By the following year a further 14 squadrons were operating Hurricanes (including the Indian Air Force). And it is probably not too much to suggest that the bulk of close support and tactical reconnaissance for the advancing 14th Army during the years 1943–45 was carried out by the ubiquitous Hurricane units. The aircraft's rugged construction, superb stability and extreme versatility proved nearly ideal in the almost primitive fighting conditions of the jungle war.

In the offensive role Hurricane IIBs and IICs, bearing clutches of high explosive bombs and rockets to supplement their gun and cannon armament, proved to be deadly effective close support to the jungle-bound infantry. As will be seen in the account following, the critical Allied stand at Imphal—which, with the legendary siege at Kohima, was to be the key turning point of the campaign in Burma—owed a large part of its success to air

support, provided as ever by the sturdy Hurricanes. By late 1944 most Hurricanes in Burma were being replaced by the seven-ton Thunderbolt fighters, yet on VJ-Day (August 15th, 1945) three RAF squadrons (17, 20 and 28), plus eight Indian Air Force squadrons—all battle-hardened veterans of the Far East war—were still flying Hurricanes. Thus from September 3rd, 1939 until the last day of the global war, Hurricanes served in a first-line operational capacity.

The account which follows was originally written by Flight Lieutenant E. D. C. Lewis in 1945, and describes his opinion of the work of the Hurricanes during the Imphal siege of March–April 1944. Imphal reputedly the original home of polo, stands centrally in a wide plain and athwart the main route from Burma to India. Its

Left: Beat-Up. A trio of Hurricanes of 258 Squadron beating up the remainder of the unit's aircraft, probably when the unit was based in Ceylon, 1942. Nearest two Hurricanes are BN125 and HV774 (S).

Below: Canadian pilots of 30 Squadron at Ratmanala, Ceylon, in August 1942. From left: Sgt C. I. Nuttbrown, Plt Off D. A. McDonald, Sgt Jack Hurley, Plt Off Jimmy Whalen (killed in action April 18th, 1944), Sgts Grant Bishop, G. Murray and G. G. Bate. The aircraft is Hurricane BG827, (RS-W), named *Bitsa*, the personal aircraft of Jimmy Whalen at the time.

Above left: Fine aerial view of a Hurricane IIc (minus its cannons) in Bengal skies. Judging by the markings, and lack of armament, this was probably a training machine.

Right: Fighter Leader. Wing Commander Frank Carey, of whom an official historian wrote: "He was the back-room boy of the Burma victory in air supremacy, the man whose refresher courses in gunnery and tactics at his school (the Air Fighting Training Unit, Calcutta) produced some of the most ingenious fighter pilots of the war. In Burma it was said that a remarkable proportion of enemy fighters brought down were destroyed by pilots listening to the echo of Carey's voice and obeying his teaching.' Carey's final war tally of victories has never been fully confirmed, a minimum figure of 28 being usually quoted, though reliable evidence suggests this figure is far below his real tally.

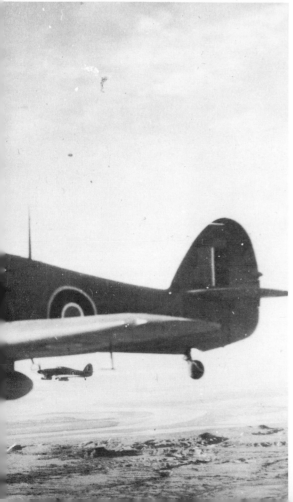

heroic defence was partly responsible for nullifying the Japanese intended invasion of India.

During the siege targets were almost in Imphal itself and many were north of the Manipur capital, indicative of the seriousness of the threat from that direction. With the clearing of the Japs from that area, the Battle of the Tiddim Road got under way. The progress of the army could be followed by noting the movement of line from milestone to milestone as one after another the enemy pockets of resistance were obliterated. Then the 40-hairpin bend—the 'Chocolate Staircase'—was dealt with, followed by Tiddim, the much-bombed Vital Corner, Kennedy Peak No 3 Stockade, Fort White, the Hurribombers cleared the way for the army. Brief one-line sentences announce nonchalantly, 'All bombs in target area. Fires started. Fires spreading. Explosions seen.'

Bridges, transports, troops, foxholes,

Left: Close Escort. A Hurricane IIc tucks in close to its bomber 'charge' during a raid among the Burmese hills.

Bottom right: Indian fighter. Hurricanes of the Indian Air Force (the prefix 'Royal' was not conferred until March 1945), fitted with long-range fuel tanks—the virtual backbone of Tac-R missions in Burma. Built up solely as a tactical air force, the IAF seldom received any of the more 'glamorous' aspects of the Burma air war; yet the total of merely nine squadrons (all types of duty) flew over 16,000 operational sorties and 44 members were decorated for superlative gallantry and services. At least 50 IAF pilots were lost in action over Burma alone, apart from other casualties.

135

Top right: Recce. A reconnaissance patrol Hurricane crosses the Irrawaddy River, alongside the Aya Bridge, in Mandalay, whilst 'scouting' for the 14th Army.

Right: Calcutta Guard—YB-L of 17 Squadron lifts off Red Road, Calcutta—an unorthodox, if practical runway.

Far right: Another mission Starts. Flying Officer J. H. Slimon, RCAF, takes off on the Arakan front, July 7th, 1943. Only two of the usual four cannons are fitted—a slight boost to performance and handling qualities.

supply dumps were destroyed, and hundreds killed in the monsoon months that the enemy had calculated on as a rest and rehabilitation period. From the beginning of March and on through the monsoon, the Hurricanes had only missed hitting the enemy on a small number of days. In that vital period, nearly $5\frac{1}{2}$ million pounds of bombs were delivered with pinpoint accuracy in the course of 12,252 sorties. The greatest effort of any month came in April, when the enemy regarded Imphal as a halting place on the road to Delhi. Over 1 million pounds of bombs raised the first doubt as to whether their destination would be reached. The army displayed an enthusiasm for Hurri-bombers as of no other combat aircraft in the India–Burma theatre. From the despatches of commanding generals to the private mail of the men fighting in the jungle, have come messages of praise for Hurri-bomber attacks pressed

home at the appropriate moment. It is the proud boast of the pilots that they have never failed to give prompt aid when called upon by their comrades fighting on the ground. Indeed, one of the squadrons, which stayed in the valley through the siege, is proud of the number of 'strawberries' it has received from the army and other sources arising out of its most successful partnership. Today the army has come to look upon the Hurri-bombers as an extremely adaptable artillery arm hitting the enemy at long range or within a few yards of the British front line, whichever hurt him most. The vast majority of bombs dropped have been 250 pounders, but that eggs of double the weight could be carried over the treacherous mountain terrain and through some of the most dangerous air currents in the world was established in July, when a small force hit the 420ft long Yanan bridge near Tamu,

an extremely vulnerable link in Jap communications, and blew out three spans.

Indian Air Force, RAF and men of the Empire air forces have piloted these formidable weapons, and, in the days when the Japanese were ringed around Imphal, were often bombing targets within five miles of their strip. Machines were serviced, re-armed and refuelled within range of enemy mortar and shell fire, and marauding parties of Japs penetrated frequently to within a few yards of the airstrip. On one occasion a patrol was surprised less than 100 yards from the pilots' sleeping quarters. Ground crews, for the first time, could watch the effect of the bombs they had risked their lives to load—in fact, the Sunday lunch-hour calm of an RAF Group HQ was once

disturbed during the siege with terrific explosions from the nearby hills. It was a Hurri-bomber squadron blasting hideouts overlooking the headquarters of the airstrip, and the diners had a grandstand view. Hurri-bomber pilots rated monsoon weather a more formidable enemy than the Japanese as they flew in and out of mountain gorges half obliterated with thick cloud to burn out some particularly troublesome strongpoint, but they were proud of the way their aircraft had stood up to the buffeting and they would readily recount how on one occasion the monsoon outsmarted them. Crews were briefed to destroy the Hpaunzeik bridge west of Kalewa. They flew to the scene and found the bridge had gone—the monsoon had got there first and destroyed it for them!

Far left: 40-Hour Inspection. Leading Aircraftmen Ivor Lillington, H. Wollett, W. 'Dusty' Miller and R. Francis overhauling a Hurricane IIc in March 1945. As in every other theatre of air operations the ground crews were a vital section of the 'team'.

Left: Overshoot. BG802, thought to be from 28 Squadron, decides to park in its own fashion, Cox's Bazaar.

Below: A mixture of uniforms and Services, in this case, 28 Squadron, typifying the supreme teamwork of all three allied Services which made final victory in Burma possible.

Men and Markings

Squadron Leader Billy Drake, DSO, DFC, with the Hurricane he flew as commander of 128 Squadron at Hastings, Sierra Leone, West Africa, winter 1941–42. The spinner was hooped in red, white and blue.

Above: Canadian John Kent, pictured when a Flight commander of the Polish 303 Squadron at Northolt, 1940. High on the Hurricane's fuselage is the 'Kosciuszko' badge carried on all 303's aircraft. Kent finished the war with a credited total of 21 victories, and eventually retired from the RAF as a Group Captain, DFC, AFC.

Top centre: The Joker. Ornate insignia of Squadron Leader John W. C. Simpson, DFC when he commanded 245 Squadron at Aldergrove, Northern Ireland, late 1940. An ex-43 Squadron pilot, Simpson was the subject of the book, *Combat Report* by Hector Bolitho.

Right: Lucky Tuck. Squadron Leader R. R. S. Tuck, DSO, DFC, when commander of 257 Squadron at North Weald, November 1940, strapped into the cockpit of Hurricane V6864, DT-A. The Burmese 'flag', a standard blue ensign, was in honour of the fact that 257 had been 'adopted' by the Burmese government (pre-Burmese independence). Tuck finished the war with a credited total of 29 victories in the air.

Right: Irish Tally. Squadron Leader J. I. Kilmartin, DFC, who fought in 1 Squadron during the 1940 French campaign, and with 43 Squadron in the latter stages of the Battle of Britain. In the spring of 1942 he succeeded Billy Drake in command of 128 Squadron in West Africa, and by 1944 was Wing Commander of a 2nd TAF Typhoon Wing. His final tally was at least 15 victories.

Bottom centre: Under Two Flags. D. L. du Vivier, a Belgian, who fought through the battles of France, Britain, North Africa, Tunisia and Italy, and survived the war. Seen here as commander of 43 Squadron (the 'Fighting Cocks') in early 1942, with a panel showing the RAF and Belgian flags and 43 Squadron's black/white dicing marking.

Below: Line-Shoot. Sergeant G. D. Robertson of 402 Squadron RCAF proudly displays his 'duck-breaker' (first victory symbol) at Rochford, September 22nd, 1941.

Left: Belgian Thistle. Captain Gerard, a former World War I pilot, standing by a Hurricane of the 2nd Escadrille, BAF, March 1940. This unit badge was a continuation of the insignia carried by the unit during the 1914–18 war.

Right: Dumbo—a Hurricane IIb's insignia on the Arakan front in Burma, July 21st, 1943. The pilots (all Canadians) are Plt Off N. M. Scott, Flt Sgt W. Thompson (who flew this aircraft) and Plt Off Lloyd Miller.

Bottom right: Flying Officer Roy Dutton poses in front of two of 111 Squadron's Hurricane Is, 1939. The unit's coding, JU, can be seen on L1730 in background. The equal-division black/white undersurfaces show to advantage.

Bottom centre: Butch the Falcon—the unit insignia of 402 Squadron RCAF at Warmwell, February 9th, 1942. Aircraft is a Hurricane IIb, AE-Q, and the NCOs Corporals Graham and T. Ryland.

Bottom left: Burma Squadron. Squadron Leader Francis J. Soper, DFM, in command of 257 (Burma) Squadron in the autumn of 1941, and a Hurricane displaying the Chinthe (Burmese effigy) which figured in the official squadron badge. With a credited total of 15 victories, Soper failed to return from a sortie on October 5th, 1941.

Above: *To the Memory of . . .* Hurricane IIc, HL844 of 94 Squadron, El Gamil, Egypt, 1942, with its dedication to Sir Alasdair MacRobert who was killed in a flying accident at the Redhill Flying Club on June 1st, 1938. Two brothers, Sir Iain and Sir Roderic, were also killed whilst flying—all three being commemorated by similar inscriptions on Hurricanes of 94 Squadron (with which unit Sir Roderic had served as a Flight Lieutenant in early 1941).

Right: *Dodie*—the girl-friend of Sergeant J. R. Scott of 402 Squadron, RCAF is suitably honoured. Warmwell, February 1942.

Below: *Our John*—another Hurricane bearing a dedic- ation to a lost son. Hurricane IIb, BN795 of 174 Squadron, with its pilot, Flt Lt J. R. Sterne, DFC at Odiham, January 1st, 1943. This was one of three Hurricanes similarly inscribed, 'presented' to the RAF by Mrs Gillan, the mother of Wing Commander John Gillan, DFC, AFC, the one-time commander of the first Hurricane unit, 111 Squadron, who was killed in action, flying Spitfire V, W3715, on August 29th, 1941.

Above: Squadron Leader G. A. Butler, DFC, who commanded 11 Squadron in Burma during the last six months of the war. The Norwegian insignia on the nose of this Hurricane is presumably a reference to the aircraft's individual 'owner'. Believed taken at Sinthe airstrip.

Left: Whatever the 'book' said, there were times when simple muscle power was more convenient. LACs R. Finney and W. Jones roll a 250lb GP bomb to *Hellzapoppin*, a Hurricane IIc, in Burma 1945.

Top centre: *The Isobelle A*— motif of Pilot Officer J. Muff's Hurricane with 28 Squadron, Burma. The pilot's Canadian origins are exemplified by the added maple leaf marking.

Above: Veterans. Hurricane pilots of 80 Squadron at Eleusis, Greece, early 1941, where they were part of the pitifully few RAF fighters who fought an outstanding air campaign against vastly superior numerical odds. From left: Plt Off 'Keg' Dowding; Plt Off 'Ginger' Still; Sgt C. E. 'Cas' Casbolt (eventually commissioned, awarded a DFM and credited with at least 13 victories); Warrant Officer M. 'Mick' Richens; Sgt E. W. F. 'Ted' Hewitt, DFM (who ended the war as a Squadron Leader with 21 victories); and Fg Off 'Twinstead' Flower.

Left: Bulldog Breed. The ferocious figure carried by a Hurricane of the RCAF, 135 Squadron, at Patricia Bay, British Columbia on January 6th, 1943.

Right: 73 Squadron pilots in France, May 1940. From left; Sgt Pilkington; Fg Off H. G. 'Ginger' Paul (15 victories); Fg Off O. 'Fanny' Orton, DFC (25 victories, killed in action September 17th, 1941); and Fg Off E. J. 'Cobber' Kain, DFC (17 victories, killed in flying accident June 1940).

Above right: Deadly Duck. An aggressive Walt Disney Donald Duck which adorned the Hurricane IIc flown by Sergeant Jack Pollock of 30 Squadron, Ceylon, July 11th, 1943.

Left: Fighting Cocks. Pilots of 43 Squadron's A Flight at Wick, 1940. From left: Sgt Buck; Fg Off C. A. Woods-Scawen, DFC (killed in action September 3rd, 1940); Flt Lt Caesar Hull, DFC (killed in action September 8th, 1940); Fg Off Wilkinson and Sgt G. W. Garton (who ended the war as a Wing Commander, DSO, DFC).

Left: False Colours. V7670 in German markings, which was recaptured on Gambut airfield, North Africa, in January 1942. Personnel here are (from left) Flt Lt Whittard, McKenny Paul Rylands.

Bottom left: False Colours. JS327, a Canadian Sea Hurricane of 808 Squadron, FAA from HMS *Chaser*, which force-landed at St Leu, Algeria on November 8th, 1942, just after the initial Operation 'Torch' Allied landings there.

Right: An Ace meets his King. Flight Lieutenant Geoffrey Allard, DFC, DFM, receives his DFC award from the hands of King George VI, at a hangar investiture, early 1941.

Below: Silver Warrior. AG244, an ex-Desert Air Force Hurri-bomber which was relegated to training duties with the Central Flying School, Norton, (No 33 FIS), Southern Rhodesia, in 1945. Finished all-silver (reminiscent of the Hurricane prototype), the rear fuselage band was in red, edged with blue. Its ignominious end came in 1948 when, with about 50 DH Tiger Moths and Airspeed Oxford trainers, it became one section of a huge bonfire. . . .

In Many Forms

Cannon Sextet. Immaculate echelon of 3 Squadron's Hurricane IIcs in 1941. Identities include: Z3069 (F); Z3092 (T); Z3094 (R); BD869 (P); Z3464 (Z); and BD867 (Y).

Above: Advanced Trainer. P3039, a Hurricane I belonging to Squadron Leader (later, Group Captain) W. D. David, DFC, whilst instructing at No 55 Operational Training Unit in 1942. Just below the engine exhaust stubs can be faintly seen the name *Joan*.

Top: Canadian Trio. Hurricane XIIs of No 1 OTU, RCAF at Bagotville, PQ, on July 31st, 1943. Nearest aircraft, 'L', is serialled 5470. Note the mini-spinners common to the majority of Canadian built Hurricanes.

Top right: Sea Boots. Early Sea Hurricane Ibs aboard a Fleet carrier.

Right: Sea Hurricane with problems. One of HMS *Argus's* brood which suffered a port wheel blow-out on landing, skidded towards the 'drink', but was saved from a dunking by the out-rigged safety nets.

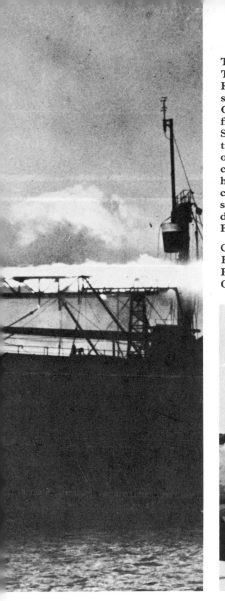

Top left: Tandem for two. The Hurricane IIc (ex-KZ232) two-seat conversion supplied to the Persian Government in 1947. First flown at Langley, on September 27th, 1946, the trainer is seen here with its original rear cockpit configuration, before the hood was modified for more comfort. Bearing the Persian serial ('2-31'). it was delivered to Doshan Teppeh FTS initially.

Centre left: Ski Boots. Hurricane XII, 5624 of the RCAF, seen at Rockcliffe, Ontario on January 1st, 1943.

Left: Catafighter. V6756, NJ-L, a Hurricane I of the Merchant Ship Fighter Unit, being blasted away from the CAM ship, *Empire Tide*.

Bottom left: Naval Threesome. Sea Hurricane 1As P3090, Z4922 and V6700—the latter having served with 504 Squadron AAF in 1940.

Below: Hurricane IIc, NF672 of 835 Squadron, FAA which hit the deck barrier of its carrier, June 27th, 1945. Just below exhaust stubs is the nickname *Nicki*.

Bottom right: Last of the Many. PZ865, the ultimate Hurricane to be produced by Hawkers, was never issued to the RAF but bought by its parent firm off contract and retained by the firm. After the war ended it was registered as a civil aircraft, G-AMAU, its armament removed and the splendid livery (seen here) of royal blue and gold was applied. Entered in several air races until 1960 (it is pictured here in September 1950), it was then repainted in military camouflage.

Requiem

A scene which was repeated
thousands of times, in
virtually every operational
theatre; pilots sprinting to
their Hurricanes for a
Scramble take-off.

Photo Credits

The illustrations in this book were obtained from the following sources:

AELR Air Museum Brussels: 26TR, 28B, 31TL, 32

Aeroplane: 67BR

Air Ministry: 127L

R.C.B. Ashworth: 41, 96L

Associated Press: 43BR

K. Atkinson: 157TR

W. Baguley: 151B

British Official: 25, 29T, 56L, 57R, 58C, 58B, 59R, 59L, 64BL, 68T, 69B, 90B, 95T, 95BR, 103TR, 110, 112T, 114B, 115T, 117B, 124, 143TR, 155B.

J. W. Brooks: 88

Charles E. Brown: 46T, 47T, 128, 156B.

J. H. F. Cutler: 135B.

J. B. Cynk: 51T, 79B.

Czechoslovak Inspectorate: 121

Group Captain W. D. David, CBE, DFC, AFC: 154B.

Air Commodore R. G. Dutton, CBE, DSO, DFC: 145BR.

F. A. Etchells: 84, 97B.

Flight International: 12T, 12B, 13T, 14, 15B, 15T, 18, 19, 20, 21, 23T, 78T.

Fox Photos: 36, 53, 61, 63, 78TR, 82B, 127R.

Graphic Photo Union: 89.

Hawker Siddeley Aviation: 11, 55, 64T, 69TR, 69C, 109TL, 109TR, 109B, 124, 156L, 157B.

D. Howley: 112B.

Imperial War Museum: 3 Frontispiece, 26TL, 26B, 29B, 31T, 31B, 38, 43T, 43BL, 50, 65T, 66T, 66B, 87, 93, 94T, 94B, 95BL, 102B, 104, 112C, 113, 115B, 116B, 117T, 118, 119TR, 119TL, 127, 131, 132TR, 134T, 134B, 135T, 136T, 138, 139B, 142T, 142B, 146TL, 147TR, 147C, 147B, 149TR, 149BR, 151T, 153, 157TL.

S. H. Ker: 139, 147TL.

Keystone Agency: 17

Squadron Leader P. G. Leggett: 96TR, 97T, 97C.

Life Magazine (Wm Vandivert): 45T.

Ministry of Information: 122T.

MOD (Air): 43CL, 91, 102T.

R. Munday: 130.

Sergeant H. Newton: 98.

Cyril Peckham, FRPS: 22.

J. Pickering: 111, 116C.

PNA Ltd: 27, 67T, 119B, 123

Public Archives of Canada: 23B, 37R, 68B, 78B, 80, 81T, 81BR, 81BL, 82TL, 85, 90T, 133B, 137, 143BR, 144BR, 145T, 146B, 148B, 149TR, 154T, 156C, 159.

M. Ross: 37L, 47B.

R. J. Ryley: 116T.

C. Smith: 132B.

F.F Smith: 114T.

6 Squadron: 101, 107.

28 Squadron: 132T.

32 Squadron: 45B.

43 Squadron: 143BL.

85 Squadron: 44

111 Squadron: 35.

Lt-Col Avi M. Terlinden, BEM: 30R.

G. T. Thomas: 136B.

Topical Agency Ltd.: 51B.

R. F. Watson: 49, 52.

R. Leask Ward: 150B.

Flight Lieutenant Whittard: 150T.

The remainder are from the Author's collection.